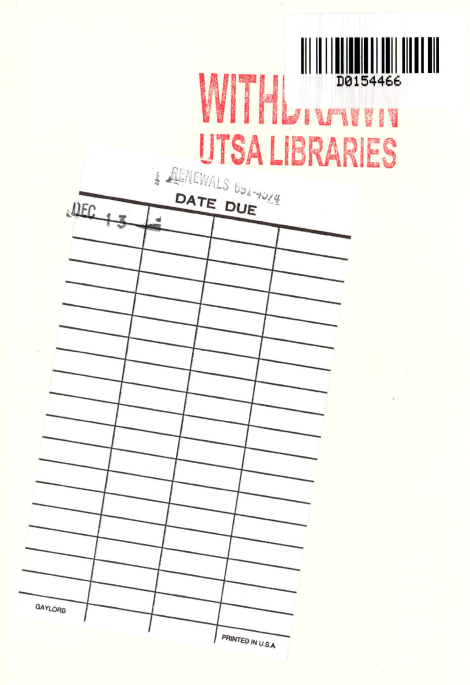

WRITING
for the
COMPUTER
SCREEN

WRITING
for the
COMPUTER
SCREEN

HILARY GOODALL
&
SUSAN SMITH REILLY

New York
Westport, Connecticut
London

Portions of Chapter Six are reprinted, with permission, from *IEEE Computer Graphics & Applications,* Vol. 4, No. 2, pp. 42-51, Feb. 1984. ©1984 IEEE.

Portions of Chapter Six are reprinted, with permission, from *Educational Technology,* Vol. 26, No. 1, pp. 36-40, Jan. 1986. © 1986 Educational Technology.

Library of Congress Cataloging-in-Publication Data

Goodall, Hilary.
 Writing for the computer screen / Hilary Goodall and Susan Smith Reilly.
  p. cm.
 Bibliography: p.
 Includes index.
 ISBN 0-275-92947-7 (alk. paper)
 1. Electronic publishing. 2. Electronic data processing—
Authorship. 3. Authorship—Data processing. I. Reilly, Susan Elizabeth Smith.
II. Title.
Z286.E43R45   1988
686.2′2—dc19   88-22447

Library of Congress Catalog Card Number: 88-22447
ISBN: 0-275-92947-7

First published in 1988

Praeger Publishers, One Madison Avenue, New York, NY 10010
A division of Greenwood Press, Inc.

Printed in the United States of America

∞

The paper used in this book complies with the Permanent Paper Standard issued by the National Information Standards Organization (Z39.48-1984).

10 9 8 7 6 5 4 3 2 1

CONTENTS

FIGURES

PREFACE

We impose the form of the old on the content of the new.
The malady lingers on.

Marshall McLuhan, 1967

There is always a period of adjustment when people impose the familiar forms of old technology on the content displayed by a new technology. Historically, theatrical forms were imposed on motion pictures and the forms of radio were imposed on television.

During a period of adjustment, the unique characteristics of the new technology emerge and a transformation occurs resulting in new forms unique to the new technology which change or enhance content. In the case of motion pictures, conventions of film making emerged that allowed the development of drama freed from the confines of real time and space. In the case of television, video production and transmission techniques emerged that created electronic news gathering, instant replay and music video.

The introduction of computers conforms to McLuhan's old adage as well. We are now in the period of adjustment between imposition of old forms on this new technology and the development of new ones. Many people still try to impose print manuscript forms on electronic text display. This book is an attempt to call attention to the emerging new forms of information display that are unique to the computer medium.

The use of computerized information continues to proliferate. More and more people are using computer display screens on their jobs. Businesses are installing internal computer networks, students are taking computers to college, professionals are subscribing to videotext services, families are buying home computers to help with financial and household chores, individuals are subscribing to electronic mail services, broadcasters are adding teletext to their programming choices. As computer use increases, so does the need to be able to create information that can be used comfortably and efficiently, without the physiological stress reported by many people.

The techniques for writing and designing computer screens presented in this book are informed by professional experience with computer display in business and in education. It is hoped this experience will serve you well.

ACKNOWLEDGMENTS

Many people have helped shape the theories of electronic text outlined in the first five chapters. Special thanks go to the teletext pioneers of CEEFAX — in particular Colin McIntyre, Ian Irving, Mort Smith and Pete Winter, who over the years have shared ideas and bottles of Sans Fils with equal liberality; to Mark Bellamah and all at ELECTRA for keeping the faith; and to Don Jensen for his help and support through the whole process — H.G.

Special thanks to Anne Bell, graphic artist, for her assistance in the design and layout of this manuscript, particularly the last two chapters; and to Jack, Sarah and Jessie Reilly for providing additional time and space for my work — S.R.

WRITING
for the
COMPUTER
SCREEN

1

IN SEARCH OF A WALL: CONCEPTS IN ELECTRONIC TEXT

Teletext veteran Colin McIntyre, who saw the British Broadcasting Corporation's CEEFAX service through its early years, has been known to point out the similarities between those involved in electronic publishing and graffiti artists: it doesn't matter what kind of wall you have to write on, so long as you have a wall. The skills learned in one branch of the industry are as valid in others. Good editing, style, and design are as relevant to a writer on a national teletext news service as to a copywriter seeking to promote soft drinks in a videotex advertisement or even the business executive trying to compile a report for a private computer network. All have to work with the possibilities and the limitations of the electronic screen.

So what is so important about electronic text? Why can't you just take newswire copy and type it onto the screen, or a newspaper advertisement and turn it into computer graphics? Surely there is no good reason why you should not start writing a marketing report exactly as if you had your trusty portable typewriter in front of you? To answer those questions, you need to put yourself in the position of those on the receiving end of the information. Sitting in front of a video display terminal (VDT) — or a television doubling as a VDT — is not one of those comfortable experiences. The screen flickers, it cannot be readily adjusted for optimum reading angle and distance, in fact, reading from the screen requires real effort and attention spans can be mercilessly short. Readers will only pursue information they see as valuable, and if you presume too far upon their patience, there is always the off switch or, in the case of pay services, the discontinued subscription.

The screen itself offers many possibilities, but it also involves some drawbacks as a communication medium. The most obvious limitation is space. Each screen can only accommodate a small number of words. The medium does not encourage browsing, nor is referring back and forward within a piece particularly easy. So each very limited screen should be largely self-contained and satisfying, which is no small achievement when dealing with blocks of about seventy-five words. Even in two-way interactive videotex with its vast page capacity, research has shown most people only read the first frame or two of an extended story. After three or four frames only a determined handful of readers is still hanging in there.

A screen jammed with words is difficult to read, while complex sentence structure, jarring color combinations, and an alphabet soup of abbreviations all reduce the reader's receptiveness to the message you are trying to communicate. This new medium has raised all kinds of questions about the way the eye scans a page and assimilates information. People still need coaxing to accept the idea of reading from their television screens.

The opportunities offered by electronic publishing make it more than worthwhile to overcome the obstacles. One significant advantage is the speed with which news and other information can be brought to the reader. Real time news and the ability to update a running story as often as necessary are great assets. The rigorous editing dictated by space limits often increases the vitality of a story — or any other piece of writing — and makes the facts rapidly and easily accessible.

Videotex and teletext readers basically put together their own newspaper, financial magazine, or sports digest by selecting the pages they want to read and only those pages. A sense of participation in the news process creates a strong relationship between readers and the service. Some self-appointed proofreaders like to keep editors on their toes at the ELECTRA teletext newsroom in Cincinnati. Drop a category of page or play around with the format and you risk angering untold legions of devotees. In an article in the *Quill,* Don Sider, who led Time Inc.'s teletext project, is quoted as saying: "You are not a viewer. You are not a passive voyeur of the TV screen. You are a participant here. You have a keypad in hand.... We find that people are becoming almost passionate in their feelings about what they like and dislike" (Aumente, 1983).

Electronic publishing ventures fall into three broad categories — videotex, teletext, and cabletext. As the names imply, they all offer pages of text, although the applications, technical specifications, and means of transmission vary widely. All three kinds of computer-based information service are currently available in the United States. There are many different technical standards and degrees of sophistication — some services use no color or graphics, some use color and simple mosaic graphics, while others have the potential to transmit photographic quality pictures along phone wires or over the airwaves.

Videotex is used interchangeably with electronic publishing as a generic term for the industry as a whole. It is also the term used for two-way interactive services. Subscribers are linked to a central database by phone line or occasionally by two-way cable and can access thousands of pages of information directly from that database. They can also talk back to the computer — replying to questionnaires, ordering goods, playing games, and in some cases leaving messages in electronic mailboxes for other subscribers. Usually, videotex services charge a subscription fee and hourly connection charges. Subscribers need either a home computer or a dedicated terminal to access the videotex service.

Teletext is a broadcast service. A limited number of pages — usually no more than 200 — is transmitted in a continuous cycle using a portion of the regular television signal called the vertical blanking interval or VBI. Several thousand pages can be broadcast using all 525 lines of a cable channel. Teletext appears to be interactive, in that readers can call up the pages of their choice using a keypad but they do not directly access the database. The reader needs a decoder to grab the pages from the broadcast cycle and display them on the screen. Once the reader has a television set with teletext capabilities or an add-on adapter, teletext is generally a free service.

Cabletext provides pages of text and sometimes graphics, which appear one after another on spare cable channels or on television stations during breaks in regular programming. The viewer has no control over which pages appear or how long they remain on the screen. Viewers do not require any special equipment to receive cabletext other than a regular television. The services are generally free to the viewer.

The editorial content is as varied as the technical standards. Some services offer news or sports, others bring you detailed statistics from the world of high finance, while others allow you to go electronic shopping from the comfort of your computer terminal. But when it comes to writing effectively or designing appealing pages, the same basic principles apply regardless of the specifics of the individual service.

Some areas of electronic publishing are fairly well established, while others are in their infancy. Such on-line data services as the Dow Jones/News Retrieval Service, Compuserve, and The Source pioneered the industry in the United States. Originally conceived as computer timesharing services, they have added information packages, computer shopping, electronic mail, and many other services. Subscribers need a computer, a modem, and a certain level of computer literacy to access the services. For a monthly service fee and connection charges, subscribers can follow the news, join bulletin boards, or even order airline tickets. Such services offer a no-frills, text-only format, which has proved attractive to the business user.

Other two-way videotex ventures have tried to take the risk of technological trauma out of their services. Through the use of dedicated terminals, not unlike remote television controllers, service operators have sought to entice even ardent twentieth-century Luddites to try out videotex. Viewtron in Florida, Gateway in California, and Keycom in Chicago all tried to tempt the home consumer — and advertiser — with color, sophisticated graphics, and as much pizzazz as the screen could muster. So far the U.S. consumer has voted with the pocketbook against the glamor and glitz approach. The trend in the industry has been back to basics.

Two-way interactive videotex has had a slow start all over the world because systems are expensive to run and have yet to make a significant impact on the home consumer. Britain's Prestel was the world's first true videotex service. Back in 1979 it was seen as a way to encourage residential customers to use their phones more outside business hours — it is no coincidence that Prestel is owned by British Telecom, the national phone service. After a couple of disappointing years Prestel switched its focus, and now its subscriber base is largely in the business community and among small specially targeted groups, such as computer hobbyists.

France and West Germany both have extensive videotex systems. The French Minitel service was originally seen as a way to replace telephone directories with videotex terminals. To increase penetration, the government has subsidized the cost of terminals, while gradually the service has expanded to include other information providers. West Germany's Bildschirmtext is one of the most advanced videotex systems. It offers a comprehensive selection of information and transactional services using a sophisticated network of computers.

Many of these large videotex services farm out responsibility for parts of their databases to outside information providers (IPs). Some of these IPs are large companies themselves with established expertise in communications. Publishing giant Gannett, the Associated Press, the Official Airline Guide, and Compustore are among the major U.S. videotex information providers. But the market is not just open to large players. In the foreseeable future any creative individual with a home computer and a modem could become an IP. There are already people offering tailor-made packages of show-business news, horoscopes, and at one time there was even a lurid videotex soap opera. Small-scale IPs could be the cottage industry of the information age.

Two-way interactive videotex may be the most talked about part of the electronic publishing industry, but teletext is probably the most widely used. At the last count, twenty-eight different countries had some kind of teletext service. Teletext began in Britain when some BBC engineers wanted to put information for the hearing impaired into an unused portion of the television signal. Those on the programming side did not take long to appreciate the wider potential — and so CEEFAX was born. Britain now boasts some five million teletext households and text services on all four national networks. The commercial network's ORACLE service has shown teletext can be an advertising success, and the fourth network has pioneered alternative teletext programming. Channel 4's 4-Tel service has foresworn the traditional news format in favor of information to supplement the network's video programming.

Teletext is flourishing all over Europe, Australia, and parts of the Far East. It is a part of daily life used to check news headlines, sports scores, TV schedules, and travel information. Switzerland has three different networks catering to the three main language groups within the country. Seven-Tel in Australia has become the main source of betting information because of its automated links to the state-run off-track betting service. In Austria the teletext computer system is linked with Vienna airport's computer and can give up-to-the-minute information on flight arrivals and departures.

In the United States teletext is just beginning to establish itself. The two main teletext operations are ELECTRA and Tempo Text. ELECTRA is a general-interest news service distributed nationally along with the signal of Superstation WTBS, while Tempo Text is a stock-quote service aimed at the business community. Several specialized services are aimed at agribusiness and satellite dish owners. In the future it seems likely that teletext operations will become as diverse as radio stations now are, with several services in each market — one offering news, one sports, another business information or classified advertising or even educational programming for children.

Cabletext is sometimes simply a cycle of teletext pages turned into a video picture and screened on a spare cable channel or used instead of a test pattern at times when TV stations do not have regular programming. For over a year Keyfax in Chicago aired an overnight cabletext service called Nite Owl on WFLD. Editors at the Keyfax teletext operation would put together a special sequence of pages for use on the station between sign-off and sign-on. Other organizations produce frames solely for use in cabletext. The Associated Press markets a service called AP News Plus for cable operations, and there are countless smaller services, such as the one generated at the University of Florida's Electronic Text Center.

Corporate videotex is another fast-growing part of the electronic publishing industry. It applies the principles of commercial systems to a closed network for business use. Videotex allows users with little computing experience to access information simply and efficiently. The information can be updated whenever necessary, and sensitive documents can be protected by a system of passwords.

U.S. automaker Buick has a very successful private videotex system called EPIC. Among other functions, EPIC can give dealerships up-to-date information on inventory, stock locations, and factory orders, as well as calculating financing (Aubry, 1985). Computer giants IBM and Digital Equipment Corporation are just two of the many corporations that have built extensive private videotex systems to improve the flow of information between their offices all over the country.

Electronic mail is a similar concept, although much more limited. People hooked up to a computer network or videotex service, such as Compuserve or The Source, can send and receive electronic messages via their computer. Messages can be anything from a love poem to a technical report to a reminder that your cat has an appointment at the vet's. In many cases the content will dictate the form, but the principles involved in electronic publishing may be useful for enhancing the effectiveness of the message and sparing the recipient from lengthy spells in front of the screen.

Laser disk technology is opening up new vistas for electronic publishing. Compact disks (CDs)—until recently confined to the stereo rack — are being used to store massive amounts of computer information. In the same way that a regular CD has music recorded on it, a CD ROM (Read Only Memory) carries recorded information — with more than enough room to store the contents of a large book. Despite the huge storage capacity of laser disks, the display characteristics outlined for videotex are still applicable. The CD ROM could well be the perfect vehicle for the electronic encyclopedia and other reference works, but the material will need the same kind of editorial treatment as a videotex news story. It will need to be reworked and compressed if it is to succeed on the screen, for few people will want to spend hours reading through complex electronic text.

A successful electronic publishing industry is already spawning a new segment of the advertising industry. Many advertising agencies both in the United States and Europe have departments devoted to supplying material for videotex and teletext. In Britain teletext advertising is no longer considered "experimental"; it is just another part of the media mix. One thing has become clear from the British experience: it is unwise simply to translate accepted lore from newspaper, magazine, or television advertising to electronic publishing. Videotex and teletext have their own special strengths, and gradually advertisers are discovering the best way to play up those strengths. Advertisers can benefit from the ability to present timely information and update it rapidly. Electronic publishing can give detailed information about products and services, as well as phone numbers to place orders — or in the case of two-way videotex, consumers can place an order right there and then. Videotex advertising is not likely to be a threat to the traditional media, but rather a powerful supplement.

Electronic publishing, already an established part of life in millions of households and businesses around the world, is gaining ground in the United States. Richard Levine of the Dow Jones/News Retrieval Service remarked at the Videotex '82 convention, "The challenge today in electronic publishing is to prepare material specifically for electronic delivery and I don't think any of us are absolutely certain of the way to proceed" (Levine, 1982). Practitioners in this comparatively new art have found themselves making up their own rules as they go along, with trial and error the predominant methodology. This book aims to look at some of those trials — and errors — and shed some light on the do's and don'ts of presenting information for display on the electronic screen.

2

HOW TO COME TO GRIPS WITH THE MIDDLE EAST IN 75 WORDS OR LESS: EDITING FOR THE COMPUTER SCREEN

When sent out to cover a story, rookie reporters are told to imagine what they would tell a friend about the demonstration, court case, or flower show in question. Those are the details that make a story sing and dance. In teletext and videotex, you tend to think in terms of what you would tell that same friend during a peak-rate international phone call. Extraneous details are expensive luxuries, but the whole conversation becomes pointless if you miss out crucial facts or the story is confused. The aim is still to make the story come alive, but with brevity right up there on the priority list.

Electronic publishing is an editor's medium. The editor has to write the tightest copy possible without sacrificing clarity along the way and to do so in the shortest possible time. As Peter Winter writes, "With videotex, there is neither the room nor the time for the 'glibberish' of television, the concocted drama of the tabloids, the stilted formality of the 'serious' press or the hyperbole of advertising and marketing" (Winter, 1985).

The average teletext and cabletext story takes up one page or screen. Major stories can often spread over several pages and in the case of teletext may include multiframe cycles — several frames on the same page number that turn automatically. Two-way videotex with its larger page capacity has the option of spreading stories over as many screens as deemed desirable, although much of the available research suggests a sharp drop-off in readership after a couple of pages.

Most electronic screens can comfortably hold between seventy-five and one hundred words. Actual screen dimensions vary — some accommodate forty characters by twenty rows, some thirty by sixteen or forty by twenty-four or eighty by sixteen. Whatever the exact character count, you can expect about two average newspaper paragraphs to fit on one screen. That calls for tight editing and skillful organization if the resulting story is to be meaningful and easily read.

An editor has to be ready to pare a story down to its bare essentials, ruthlessly eradicating all fluff and puff. Every idea and every word must be made to count. When you concentrate on using clear, concise language, wooly-minded muddle gets tossed out along with excess verbiage. But editing for the electronic screen involves more than just a tight writing style. It is also an organizational process — choosing the most important facts, getting rid of repetition and organizing the flow of a piece.

When confronted with a piece of news copy — or other information — to be turned into electronic text, it is important to resist the initial temptation to dive straight in and start typing. Read the story through carefully and decide what are the most important ideas in the piece. Take the single most important fact and incorporate that into a simple, direct lead: "President Reagan says he will veto any budget bill that includes cuts in defense spending" or "Stock prices are plunging on Wall Street for a third straight day." From there you can go on to outline the impasse over the budget or the full financial horrors on the stock market, including details and comments to back up the lead.

In any story designed for another medium, there are inevitably some things that cry out for the blue pencil. Stories written for newspapers often include in-depth background information that does not fit well on a medium aiming to be succinct. Radio and TV stories often have "soft" introductions: "There's good news on the economic front." "Some local children are enjoying an unexpected day off school." The videotex version can dispense with such pleasantries and get straight down to the story on the gross national product or the gas leak at a local school. You should structure your thoughts to avoid repetition within the story. Newspaper and broadcast style both make use of repetition and recapitulation as integral parts of their presentation. Ideally, videotex does not.

Writing a videotex story is not unlike writing a lead for a newspaper story. A few words will not convey the full complexity of a story, so you have to limit yourself to the most significant facts. Once you have decided on the two or three most important points, make sure you get them across. It is always easier to start with the bare bones and add information than try to subtract details once you have incorporated them into a piece. Every editor has agonized over ways to keep some succulent — but inessential — detail in a story. In the sad saga of Conan the lobster, you do not really miss the postmortem results or the details of his rescue from the dinner table, though it took a while to accept they would not fit (see Figure 2.1).

Videotex editors cannot go far wrong if they concentrate on the central issues: the who, what, when, where, and why of a story. But you have to make sure all those issues are addressed. Working closely with the news, it is hard to understand that someone could conceivably come home from work at 6:00 p.m. and not know there had been a nuclear reactor meltdown that morning. You cannot assume knowledge on the part of the reader, and so you must retain vital background information. If essential facts are missing, it does not matter how elegant the prose or how carefully crafted the page; it is a bad story. Occasionally, even seasoned writers leave out the crucial words "South African" from reports of government forces clashing with black funeral goers. In media terms, you would be dealing with

Figure 2.1 — *Conan the Lobster*

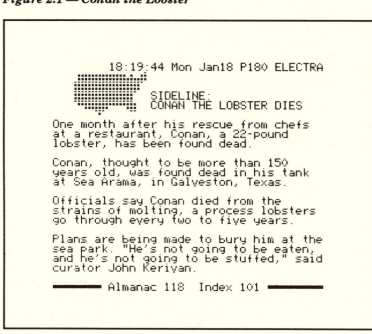

One month after his rescue from chefs at a restaurant, Conan, a 22-pound lobster, has been found dead.

Conan, thought to be more than 150 years old, was found dead in his tank at Sea Arama, in Galveston, Texas.

Officials say Conan died from the strains of molting, a process lobsters go through every two to five years.

Plans are being made to bury him at the sea park. "He's not going to be eaten, and he's not going to be stuffed," said curator John Kerivan.

Used with permission of Great American Broadcasting.

an entirely different story if the dateline were Washington instead of Johannesburg.

Always opt for hard facts rather than anecdotal material or quotes. Newspaper stories often home in on a particular individual's story, before broadening out to deal in general terms with a survey on poverty in the United States or the discovery of a new drug. It is an effective way to grab a reader's interest, but without the space to give all the details that tell the human side of the story, much of the effect is lost. Videotex writers should try to keep to the hard facts. Quotes are another problem area. You can invariably save space by paraphrasing what a witness or an expert has to say on any given issue. Small snippets of a quote often fail to convey the intended mood; they simply take up space and disrupt the flow of the story.

Organize your information. Think in terms of how you can best convey your message before starting in. A good editor will make the most of the screen's ability to use color and graphics to enhance the message. If you have a lot of statistics in a story, consider making them into a separate graph or table to accompany the written story. The videotex format is perfect for sidebars and simple graphic representation. Rather than burden a page with strings of figures, you can often get the facts across more meaningfully using a chart or graph. For example, when the unemployment figures come through each month, there is an obvious story on the overall trend, what has influenced the trend, and what it means. But when it comes to the details of state-by-state figures or a breakdown of the statistics by age, sex, and race, a table or graph can give a much clearer picture than pages of text. Tabulated baseball scores are easier to take in at a glance than a report that basically lists the results of the games. A map showing the location of a plane crash is much better than half a page of text trying to describe exactly where the aircraft went down.

The space limitations of the electronic screen can create severe headaches for the responsible editor. Only the foolhardy would try to condense the problems of the Persian Gulf into seventy-five words, but sometimes that is exactly what one is called on to do. Often the only sensible approach is to separate out the various strands of a story and present each one as an individual story. Don Sider, who presided over Time Inc.'s teletext project, aptly described the editing philosophy: "Short blocks of information do best — it is almost like cutting up someone's steak for them. It's got to be digestible" (Aumente, 1983). Attaining digestibility often involves extracting the salient points from a mass of information designed for other media, then refining, reshaping, and often totally rewriting for the electronic screen.

Taking the Persian Gulf as an example, when fighting flares, there are many stories that could be written:

1. Claims and counterclaims from Iran and Iraq about what ships have been hit and by whom;
2. What U.S. forces in the Gulf are doing in response;
3. Efforts by the United Nations to achieve a cease-fire;
4. Reaction by U.S. and world leaders;
5. Background including a chronology of the war and details of U.S. involvement in the Gulf;
6. The effect of the fighting on the world oil market, gold prices, and the U.S. stock market.

Each one of these stories adds to the overall picture of what is happening in the Gulf War and what it means. But each story must also be able to stand alone. A reader might just want to know about the U.S. response and call up only that page, in which case it must be complete and satisfying on its own. But the page must also work as one part of the whole series of stories. The great challenge to the editor of a multipage piece is to compose a story of building blocks that can be totally rearranged and still make perfect sense.

The trend toward several short stories rather than one long report can be seen in newspapers too. USA Today has pretty much perfected the art of the sidebar. Dividing up a complex story makes it easy to understand, but you have to be careful how you divide it. Readers have to absorb information one screen at a time, so do not increase their work load by referring back to previous pages.

In videotex, multipage stories are usually stored in streams that are accessed by pressing the MORE or NEXT key. Teletext offers two basic kinds of multipage story. Individual stories can be given separate page numbers, or a series of cycling frames can share one page number. The reader has to call up the individual stories, while the frames cycle automatically when given one page number. In all cases, each screenful of text should be self-contained (see Figure 2.2).

Figure 2.2a — Dracula: Multipage Story

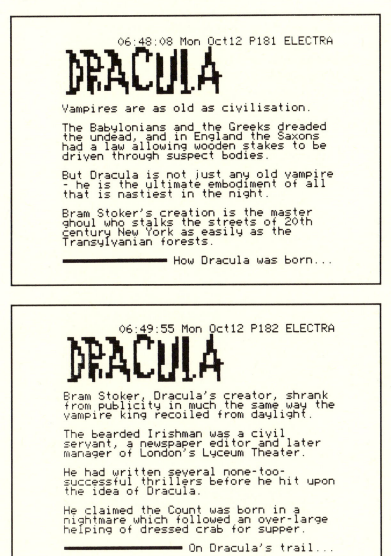

Used with permission of Great American Broadcasting.

Figure 2.2b — Dracula: Multipage Story

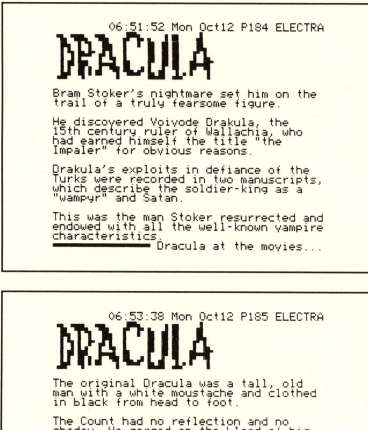

06:51:52 Mon Oct12 P184 ELECTRA

DRACULA

Bram Stoker's nightmare set him on the trail of a truly fearsome figure.

He discovered Voivode Drakula, the 15th century ruler of Wallachia, who had earned himself the title "the Impaler" for obvious reasons.

Drakula's exploits in defiance of the Turks were recorded in two manuscripts, which describe the soldier-king as a "wampyr" and Satan.

This was the man Stoker resurrected and endowed with all the well-known vampire characteristics.
━━━━━━━━━━ Dracula at the movies...

06:53:38 Mon Oct12 P185 ELECTRA

DRACULA

The original Dracula was a tall, old man with a white moustache and clothed in black from head to foot.

The Count had no reflection and no shadow. He gorged on the blood of his victims but his power ceased at sunrise which would find him reposing in his coffin.

The black cloak was introduced by Hamilton Deane who first brought the vampire to the stage in 1924. The now-famous fangs were added by Christopher Lee in the 1959 Hammer film.
━━━━━━━━━━ Dracula on stage...

Used with permission of Great American Broadcasting.

Figure 2.2c — Dracula: Multipage Story

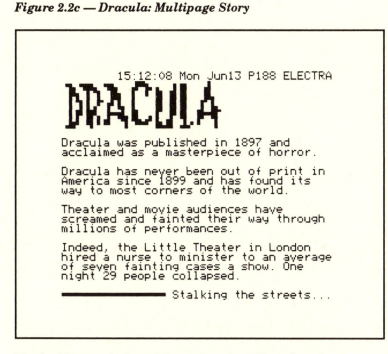

Used with permission of Great American Broadcasting.

Multiframe cycles can extend the scope of a teletext story, but they also present one of the toughest editing jobs in electronic publishing. As an editor, you have no way of knowing which frame in the cycle will appear first on the reader's screen. The best tactic is to use the principles of the regular multipage story — divide up the story and devote each frame to a separate issue. If each frame can stand alone, there are no problems with the display sequence. Multiframe cycles are very useful for such stories as a business report requiring a graph or a series of movie review capsules. A report on a presidential address could devote each frame to a separate topic — superpower relations, the budget, the Middle East, the Supreme Court nomination — creating a truly seamless circle.

Multipage stories allow electronic newspapers to give more than bare-bones headline coverage to important events, but they should not be seen as an easy option for an editor unwilling to edit. You have to be ready to take a story apart and then totally rework it. One important part of the task is writing effective teases. Readers should be encouraged to call up related pages or keep watching a cycling sequence. You should always tell them what is coming next in a cycle or where they can find further information. Hence the tease on the first page of a cycle on a presidential address might read "Comments on budget follow..." or the tease on a page about attacks on oil tankers in the Persian Gulf might read "U.S. ships on alert....See 104."

Separating out the various strands of a complex story has distinct advantages for both the reader and the editor. The reader finds the story easier to follow, and the editor finds it easier to update. By keeping the various threads of the story separate, when something changes, you just have to update one page. Without compartmentalization, an editor might have to rewrite the whole of a long, complex piece. It is faster and much less daunting to tackle just one seventy-five-word segment of a story.

Milton — not generally noted for his pithy prose — hit the mark when he wrote "Suspense in news is torture." Speed and continuous updating are the keys to success in electronic publishing. Every major videotex study has shown a direct correlation between the frequency with which information is updated and the frequency with which it is accessed. There is a certain thrill for both the journalist and the reader in following the news as it happens.

Following a running story is one of those profoundly exhilarating and at the same time exasperating experiences. From the moment the bulletin buzzer sounds, a breaking story can be on the air in a couple of minutes. Editors should not scorn to offer two paragraphs with a message saying "More details as they become available." As more information emerges, you can fill out the outline and perfect the stylistic purity of the piece.

A hijacking is the epitome of the running story. The very word can make even the most jaded electronic journalist sit up and

take notice. Teletext can follow through from the first sketchy —
and often downright inaccurate — details to the final drama of
the aircraft being stormed or the hijacker's surrender. Usually,
it takes hours for anyone to figure out exactly what is going on,
how many people are on board a hijacked jet, or who the
hijackers are. Each change in the accepted facts and figures
involves a rewrite. You write a story saying the hijacked plane
has landed in Beirut, only to find it is back in the air heading for
Tripoli. During the course of an afternoon, editors can expect to
rewrite a hijacking story dozens of times to include the latest
information. Invariably, just when you think you have written
the definitive piece of videotex prose, something new will happen, and it is back to square one.

When the space shuttle Challenger exploded, ELECTRA
carried more than fifty different stories in a couple of hours. The
way the story unfolded is more dramatic than the average story
but not all that unusual. It provides the perfect example of a
running story (see Figure 2.3).

Response from readers suggests they enjoy watching news as
it unfolds. A rapidly changing story imposes some special responsibilities on an editor, however. Being first with the news is
heady stuff, but you have to be sure of its accuracy. You have to
be careful to give the source of unconfirmed information and
explain if there are conflicting accounts. Alarm bells should
sound every time a story involves casualty figures. Such tallies
inevitably go up and down several times before an accepted total
is reached. Until that time, it is best to be vague and talk of
dozens or scores hurt in a train crash rather than have to amend
the figures every few minutes.

Videotex coverage is not tailored around specific deadlines in
the way newspaper, TV, and even radio news coverage is. You
add to stories as the information comes in, emphasizing the
newest angle. Sometimes stories seem like a revolving door. As
a story develops, older information gets bumped down and
finally off the page.

People expect the latest news from videotex or teletext. They
expect something new on the screen each time they turn to the
service, and so sometimes it is necessary to refresh a story that

Figure 2.3a — Shuttle: Running Story

```
          18:45:38 Mon Jan18 P180 ELECTRA
   :::::::::::::::  NATIONAL
   :::::::::::::::
   :::::::::::::::  news
   :::::::::::::::
   ::::::::::::    SHUTTLE OUT OF CONTROL

An explosion on the space shuttle
Challenger has sent the craft tumbling
toward the ocean.

The shuttle veered wildly out of
control two minutes after take-off.

The initial seconds after liftoff
appeared to be normal, but one of the
ship's two solid rocket boosters
apparently detonated.

NASA spokesman Steven Nesbitt says they
are waitng for word from recovery
forces in the area of the explosion.
━━━━━   Arctic air hits Florida 119  ━━━
```

```
          18:58:42 Mon Jan18 P181 ELECTRA
   :::::::::::::::  NATIONAL
   :::::::::::::::
   :::::::::::::::  news
   :::::::::::::::
   ::::::::::::    LITTLE HOPE FOR CREW

NASA says there is little hope for the
Challenger's seven crew members after
an explosion aboard the space shuttle.

Spokesman Steven Nesbitt says the
shuttle experienced an explosion two
minutes after lift-off.

The shuttle tumbled out of control into
the ocean after the blast.

The initial seconds after liftoff
appeared to be normal, but one of the
ship's two solid rocket boosters
apparently detonated.
━━━━━━   News index 101  ━━━━━━━
```

Used with permission of Great American Broadcasting.

Figure 2.3b — Shuttle: Running Story

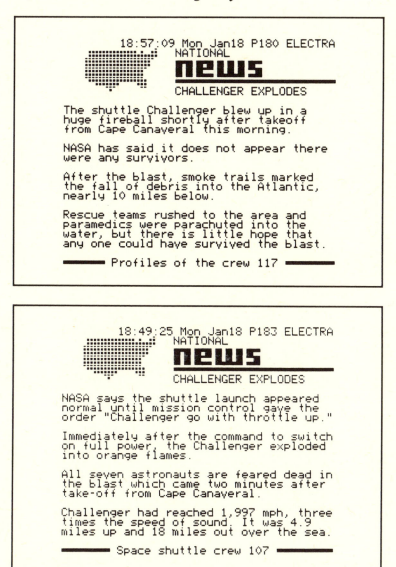

Used with permission of Great American Broadcasting.

Figure 2.3c — Shuttle: Running Story

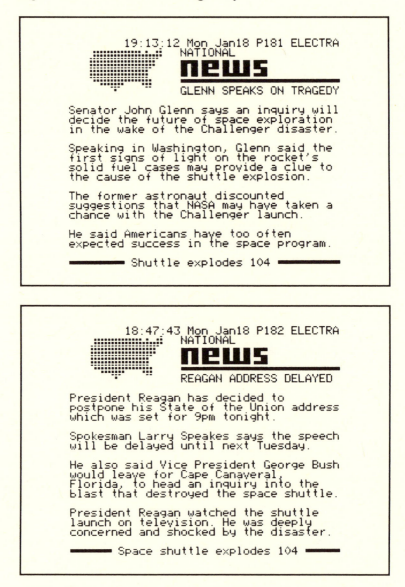

Used with permission of Great American Broadcasting.

is worth keeping but has not really developed. When no new information is available on a story and nothing better has come along to replace it, the best strategy is to take a new angle and rewrite, maybe bringing reaction to a vote in the House to the top of the story rather than leading with the vote itself.

One of hardest parts of an editor's job is deciding when to run a story, when to update it, and when to replace it. Should you keep a morning story on unrest in the Philippines or replace it with an afternoon story on a minor medical breakthrough? At what point in the day do you ditch a four-page cycle on last night's presidential address? On a busy news day do you carry separate stories on the consumer price index and retail sales figures or do you combine them in one piece?

Journalists in electronic publishing are responsible for more than just writing the news in the required format. They must also tell readers what information is available, piquing interest in pieces that might otherwise go unnoticed. Headlines pages and indexes are like the newspaper vendors who still stand on London street corners yelling, "Ferry sinks — read all about it." For all its mechanical overtones, indexing plays a vital editorial role in videotex. Imagine being in a library with no catalog and no obvious way of knowing where the one book you want is — or indeed whether the library even has it. That is the kind of feeling you get when trying to find something in an unfamiliar and badly indexed database.

Videotex databases are nonlinear. Readers have no way of knowing what is on offer unless you tell them. You could conceivably plod through 200 pages of a teletext service in search of the Dow Jones Industrial Average, but with a database of thousands of pages, the stab in the dark method would be out of the question. Most databases use some kind of tree structure of indexing. A general index lists the indexes for broad subject areas, which in turn list topic indexes or, in smaller databases, direct the reader to the contents of specific pages. Writing appealing index entries is not the most glamorous part of a videotex editor's job, but it is a vital editorial function. A great videotex page is totally wasted if no one can find it and consequently no one reads it (see Figure 2.4).

Figure 2.4 — Sports Index

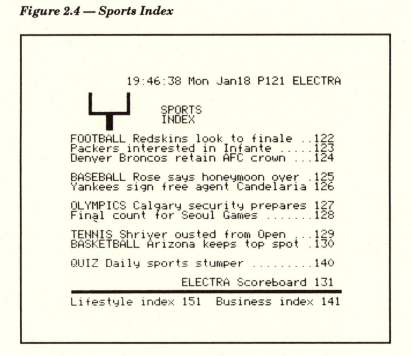

```
        19:46:38 Mon Jan18 P121 ELECTRA
              SPORTS
              INDEX
FOOTBALL Redskins look to finale ..122
Packers interested in Infante .....123
Denver Broncos retain AFC crown ...124

BASEBALL Rose says honeymoon over .125
Yankees sign free agent Candelaria 126

OLYMPICS Calgary security prepares 127
Final count for Seoul Games .......128

TENNIS Shriver ousted from Open ...129
BASKETBALL Arizona keeps top spot .130

QUIZ Daily sports stumper ........140

              ELECTRA Scoreboard 131

Lifestyle index 151  Business index 141
```

Used with permission of Great American Broadcasting.

Readers can also be led around a database by means of page links or teases. Links are created using software — for instance, a baseball story on the National League player of the week could be linked to the national league scores or standings or another baseball story. One keystroke would then call up any of those offerings. Implementing and keeping track of such links can become very complex. In large operations it is often handled by a separate team of production people.

A simpler approach is to tease the reader from one page to another. A line at the bottom of a story about a blizzard in New England might point the reader to the weather forecast. A page on Japan's booming exports might tease to the foreign exchange rates and so on. Teases offer no automatic links, but they do alert readers to related stories or arouse interest in a page that might otherwise be overlooked. Editors can get creative with teases. One memorable CEEFAX story about a truck spilling its load of haddock on a freeway referred the reader to the day's fresh fish prices.

The art of the tease is to interest the reader but without telling all. Depending on the context, these signposts can be straightforward or quirky, but they should always be scrupulously accurate. "Will Conan take the plunge?...113" might be the index entry for a story on efforts to save a 150-year-old lobster from the dinner table. "Wall Street reacts to budget plan...147" could be used at the bottom of a page on the latest round of budget talks. The basic rule is you have to deliver what you promise. Little irritates a reader more than going to the effort of calling up what is billed as this week's NFL betting odds only to find a report on an Australian tennis tournament.

The results of the editor's art should look simple. Successful stories flow easily without any sign of the effort that went into them. The reader should move effortlessly from one story to another unaware of the editing process. When talking to a class of writers, editor Arthur Plotnik remarked: "You write to communicate to the hearts and minds of others what's burning inside you — And we edit to let the fire show through the smoke" (Plotnik, 1982).

Given enough time and effort, most kinds of information can be turned into good videotex pages. Electronic text excels at handling headline news or other rapidly changing information. Stock market quotes, weather, sports, and travel information all bring out the strengths of videotex. Much of it is information that can be displayed as lists or capsules, which are especially effective on the screen (see Figure 2.5).

Short, simple pieces of information work best, but you can even find encyclopedias and mail-order catalogs on two-way videotex systems these days. The same basic principles of presentation apply regardless of the amount of information involved. The basic building block of videotex is the single screen. Encyclopedia entries need to be broken up into screen-sized chunks in

Figure 2.5 — Movie List

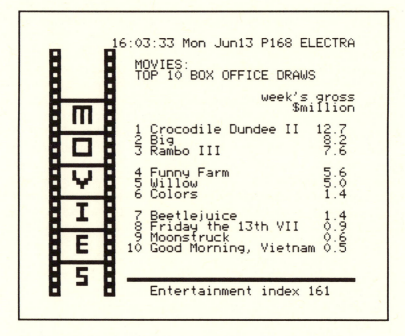

Used with permission of Great American Broadcasting.

the same way that you would approach any news story. The process is just more complicated.

Naturally, some kinds of information just do not work on videotex. Mood pieces and interviews never quite come across on the electronic screen — unless you happen to be lucky enough to interview someone who appreciates short, vivid quotes. Because of the compression needed to fit a story on a page, humor can be a problem. When you cut too much or work too hard on the words, you often end up with a forced or convoluted piece. To achieve humor, you have to ruthlessly select the facts that make the story amusing and forget the subtleties. Nor is material that depends on photographs, video, or sound for its full effect ideal for videotex. A report on a fashion show loses some of its impact without pictures of the models. Videotex can describe the basic trends — skirt lengths going up or down, the new season's colors, and so forth — but you get into deep water when you start trying to describe a nifty mid-thigh, leopard skin, halter-top number. So far, videotex advertising is largely unknown territory in the United States. Most services expect advertising will eventually foot the bill. The combination of the permanence of print and the speed of radio and TV is a potent one. Used imaginatively, the editorial strengths of videotex should also become its advertising strengths. Videotex is an excellent and relatively inexpensive medium for perishable information, such as supermarket specials, bank interest rates, and late-availability vacations. Successful advertisers will play to those strengths rather than try to convert a print ad into a rough computerized equivalent. They will give the specifications of a car or details of a special rebate rather than try to recreate a glossy photograph in computer graphics.

Inevitably, people ask, "Well who would want to call up a page of advertising?" which overlooks the fact that millions of people spend hours each Sunday poring over newspaper advertising inserts. If a page contains information that is useful to readers — be it sale bargains or commodity prices from the Chicago Board of Trade — they will call it up. Information will be the touchstone of videotex advertising. If the information is valuable, then it will be used. It is the editor's job to present the information in a way that is lively and appealing.

Videotex ads should exhibit most of the characteristics of a well produced editorial page. They can handle the same kinds of material well and should steer clear of the same danger zones. Videotex is not the medium to create the images and moods of TV commercials and magazine spreads. It is probably not even worthwhile doing ads that are little more than logos slapped on the bottom of pages. Advertisements should have information content. Videotex and teletext are great media to give a list of suppliers, prices, or a phone number to order a catalog. Two-way interactive services even offer the option of immediate purchase using the computer system and your credit card.

In videotex circles, the issue of advertising inexorably gives way to a heated discussion of the place of graphics in electronic publishing. Colin McIntyre of CEEFAX used to joke that engineers would keep on refining the graphic capabilities of teletext systems until someone had the bright idea of adding sound and making the pictures move... and then they'd call it television. When all is said and done — and usually a good deal is said on the subject — teletext, videotex, and cabletext are text media. Graphics are valuable if they enhance the text, but gratuitous decoration usually ends up irritating the reader by wasting both time, space, and in the case of two-way videotex, money in the form of connection charges.

Of course, some kinds of information can be conveyed more effectively by graphics than by text. A weather map tells you at a glance if you can expect snow in the Midwest or whether New England is experiencing a heat wave. A graph can give a great deal of easily assimilated information on the previous week's Dow Jones Industrial Average closes. When U.S. war planes bombed Libya, no one really wanted to see a drawing of an F1-11 jet, but it was helpful to use a map showing the detour the aircraft took to avoid French and Spanish air space.

On some systems graphics present an extra problem because of the amount of memory it takes to create a complex drawing and the time it takes to "paint" on the electronic screen. Designers and editors on systems that involve paint time should make sure the text appears first before the graphics start painting. At least that way you can contain the impatience of the reader. One — possibly apocryphal — story concerns a tastefully constructed page on poison treatment. The page offered emergency advice to potential poison victims but not until a graphic of a poison bottle, complete with skull and crossbones, had taken thirty long seconds to paint on the screen.

Videotex editors would do well to take to heart some words of Henry Ford: "The most beautiful things in the world are those from which all excess weight has been removed." Like the Model T, a good videotex story — stripped of all excess words, thoughts, and images — is a marvel of functional simplicity.

3

WHY VIDEOTEX EDITORS WRITE THE WORLD'S BEST POSTCARDS: STYLE FOR THE COMPUTER SCREEN

William Shakespeare noted, "Brevity is the soul of wit." It is also the guiding precept of videotex style. With about seventy-five words to tell a story, each one of those words has to count. Once you have decided what you want to say on a page, the next big question is how do you get that message across as succinctly as possible. A good page is one that successfully tells the story — a feat that usually demands clarity of thought and economy of language. The former is dealt with under editing; the latter is a question of style.

Journalists all have etched into their consciousness E.B. White's exhortation to use "definite, specific, concrete language" to maximize the impact of what they have to say (Strunk and White, 1979). It is especially important advice for those writing electronic text, as the techniques that make for vivid and powerful prose also tend to make for conciseness. Many of the following suggestions are the well worn rules of print style, while others apply specifically to the electronic screen. If there is one cardinal rule of videotex style, one edict that should be placed on every electronic keyboard, it is "Keep it short and simple."

When writers start producing copy for the electronic screen, most make the mistake of trying to pack too much information into long and involved paragraphs, reasoning that the more words you can cram onto a page the better. But each paragraph should contain only one or two sentences, and each sentence should try to convey just one idea as simply and directly as possible. Short paragraphs make pages look more inviting and are much easier to read. Keeping paragraphs down to three or four lines allows for more white space on a page. Anything longer than five lines probably needs some work.

A comparison of the two versions of the story on the Campbell's boycott is useful (see Figure 3.1). The last paragraph of the first version is complicated and confusing. The writer tried to fit too many details into one sentence and succeeded in creating an unattractive slab of text that needs reading a couple of times before it makes sense. The second version separates out the two main strands of ideas in the paragraph — the aims of the boycott and details of the dispute. This story looks better and is a good deal easier to read.

Over the past fifty years, educationalists have come up with dozens of measures of readability — how easily the language in a piece of writing can be read. Obviously, the simpler the language, the more easily people can read the piece and the greater the chance they will understand it. Pete Winter, one of the early CEEFAX pioneers, once decided to humble the literati of the teletext newsroom with a look at the reading levels required to cope with the average BBC page. Using simple mathematics and a system he called the Modified FOG Index Formula,[1] he came to the conclusion that the reading age for CEEFAX pages ranged anywhere from sixteen to twenty-five years. The average reading age in Britain is between fourteen and fifteen, while in the United States most newspapers aim their writing at eighth-grade level.

Figure 3.1 — Campbell's Boycott Story and Rewrite

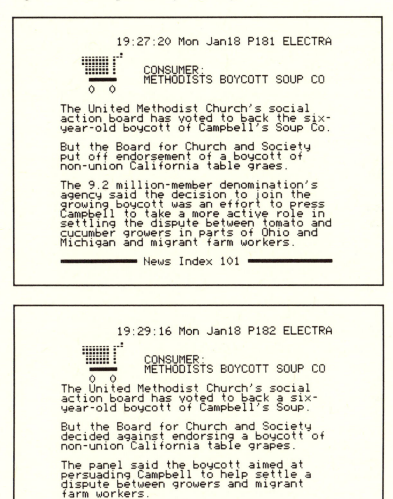

```
              19:27:20 Mon Jan18 P181 ELECTRA

     ::::::: i-:
     ::::::: i      CONSUMER:
     ━━━━━━━        METHODISTS BOYCOTT SOUP CO
      ◊   ◊

The United Methodist Church's social
action board has voted to back the six-
year-old boycott of Campbell's Soup Co.

But the Board for Church and Society
put off endorsement of a boycott of
non-union California table graes.

The 9.2 million-member denomination's
agency said the decision to join the
growing boycott was an effort to press
Campbell to take a more active role in
settling the dispute between tomato and
cucumber growers in parts of Ohio and
Michigan and migrant farm workers.
━━━━━━━━━━━━ News Index 101 ━━━━━━━━━
```

```
              19:29:16 Mon Jan18 P182 ELECTRA

     ::::::: i-:
     ::::::: i      CONSUMER:
     ━━━━━━━        METHODISTS BOYCOTT SOUP CO
      ◊   ◊
The United Methodist Church's social
action board has voted to back a six-
year-old boycott of Campbell's Soup.

But the Board for Church and Society
decided against endorsing a boycott of
non-union California table grapes.

The panel said the boycott aimed at
persuading Campbell to help settle a
dispute between growers and migrant
farm workers.

Tomato and cucumber growers in parts of
Ohio and Michigan are involved in the
dispute.
━━━━━━━━━━━━ News Index 101 ━━━━━━━━━
```

Used with permission of Great American Broadcasting.

The Modified FOG Index Formula and many other readability measures look mainly at sentence length and word length in assessing the skills — or reading age — needed to read a text with little or no difficulty. Such measures serve as a rough guide for assessing the complexity of a piece of writing. The main value of the exercise at CEEFAX came in convincing editors of the need to be more aware of the keep-it-short doctrine when it came to style. It was a source of some discomfort to discover teletext rivals at ORACLE consistently achieved lower reading ages on their stories. It should have come as no surprise, however, given that ORACLE has a house rule saying all stories should be made up of four three-line paragraphs, which in effect limits sentence length to a maximum of twenty words.

Short paragraphs are important but never more so than at the beginning of a story. Writers should try to lure the reader into a page with a crisp introduction. Many teletext services even use a different color to emphasize the crucial first paragraph. ELECTRA has a house rule outlawing introductions of more than three lines to try to ensure the lead is simple and gets directly to the point. The more accessible the language, the more likely it is that the reader will finish the story.

Short paragraphs are made up of short sentences. The key to effective writing style is keeping your sentences short and simple. Victor Hugo's novel *Les Miserables* has the distinction of containing the world's longest published sentence. At 823 words, the sentence provides enough deathless prose to fill more than ten densely packed pages of electronic text and drive even the most avid reader to distraction. Anyone writing for a videotex operation would do well to set themselves a modest twenty-five-word limit. Short, direct sentences are more manageable for the reader and often have more impact than Miltonesque strings of subordinate clauses.

The best way to deal with a rambling sentence is to separate it into two or more simple sentences. Often by restructuring the ideas, you can make the meaning clearer and even save space on the page. Sometimes it is simply a matter of modifying the punctuation.

One of the longest sentences to appear on an ELECTRA page was part of a feature on the Bulwer Lytton contest for awful writing. This sentence deservedly took the prize in 1984 and comes through with a reading age approaching thirty-two on the Winter scale:

> The camel died quite suddenly on the second day, and Salina fretted sulkily and, buffing her already impeccable nails — not for the first time since the journey began — pondered snidely if this would dissolve into a vignette of minor inconvenience like all the other holidays with Basil.

Little more than changes in punctuation bring the sentence under control, lower the reading age to twenty-two and deprive it of its true awfulness:

> The camel died quite suddenly on the second day. Salina fretted sulkily and — not for the first time since the journey began — buffed her already impeccable nails. She pondered snidely if this would dissolve into a vignette of minor inconvenience like all the other holidays with Basil.

Short sentences tend to be simple sentences. They also depend heavily on verbs — the most powerful parts of any language. Where possible, let the verb do most of the work in a sentence, as this gives vitality. Avoid using nouns where you could use a verb instead to carry the meaning. The first sentence that follows has more punch than the second:

> The Transportation Department is urging all fifty states to implement seat-belt laws.

> The Transportation Department is urging the implementation of seat-belt laws by all fifty states.

Use active verbs. Active verbs bring vigor to the language, they involve less complicated sentence structure, and they usually save space. Too many passive constructions can make even the most exciting subject read like the methodology of a physics experiment. The first sentence that follows is much shorter and crisper than the second:

Leading New York banks have cut the prime rate.

The prime rate has been cut by leading New York banks.

You can turn around almost any sentence to avoid a passive construction, although occasionally you might want to abandon the active voice for the sake of emphasis. In the following example, the first sentence is more to the point than the second:

President Reagan has been shot and wounded.

John Hinckley, Jr., has shot and wounded President Reagan.

Make your stories sound current. In news writing you should aim to use the present tense where possible or the perfect tense when dealing with a specific event that happened in the past. Using the present or perfect tense gets around the need to slip today into every story. It saves space, repetition, and on a national service, it saves the risk of confusing readers in different time zones. In both of the following examples, the first sentence is better for videotex than the second:

Senators are demanding new cuts in defense spending.

Senators today demanded new cuts in defense spending.

Senators have rejected the latest budget proposal.

Senators today rejected the latest budget proposal.

Choose simple words. There is no intrinsic merit in using long, obscure terms. Jargon, foreign phrases, and technical terms should be ruthlessly eradicated from news reports. Jargon often creeps into news copy, rendering it at best confusing and at worst incomprehensible. It is no accident that journalists translated NASA's "extra-vehicular activity" into spacewalk. Desk editors have all encountered the horrors of council-speak, of planners talking about something deemed "detrimental to the visual amenity," when they meant the proposed skyscraper would spoil the view.

Adjectives and adverbs tend to fall by the wayside in videotex. Videotex is not the place for those who hanker after the liberty of New Journalism. The format can be restricting and frustrating, but when it works, it is immensely satisfying. Some people argue the repetitive use of simple sentences creates a style that lacks sophistication and variety. Admittedly the scope for literary flourishes is limited on a seventy-five-word page, but a clear, concise style is powerful in its own right. An editorial from the New York Sun in 1890 puts it best: "It isn't the way the words are strung together that makes Lincoln's Gettysburg speech immortal, but the feelings that were in the man. But how do such little words manage to keep their grip on such feelings? That is the miracle" (*UPI Reporter*, 1983).

Word limits are a real problem in videotex. Radio or television newscasters can always talk a little faster — you only have to listen to the average sports reporter to realize how much it is possible to cram into forty-five seconds. But in videotex you are dealing with fixed dimensions and a fixed number of characters. When students on a videotex course were told to set their typewriter margins to a maximum of thirty-nine characters and write a news story as though they were writing on a screen, most tried to sneak in an extra letter or two in the hope no one would notice. Unfortunately, the screen does not suffer from human error and cannot be persuaded to let that fortieth character go by. You have to rewrite.

"But it won't fit..." is the oft-heard lament of newsroom newcomers. They suggest dispensing with periods at the end of sentences or look accusingly at the style guide or assume they made a major misjudgment in their choice of career. There are occasions when everyone has their doubts, but it is possible to make any story fit without doing violence to the meaning or the language — sometimes it just takes a while.

On good days everything fits perfectly on the thirty-nine-character line. On bad days, you always need to squeeze names like British Prime Minister Margaret Thatcher (forty characters) on the first line of a story. Try turning the piece of UPI copy in Figure 3.2 into a teletext story. The ground rules are:

1. Lines can contain no more than thirty-nine characters.
2. The first paragraph can be no more than three lines long.
3. Paragraphs can be no more than five lines long.
4. The whole story can be no more than fifteen lines long, including a blank line between paragraphs.

Figure 3.2 — Thatcher: UPI Copy

```
LONDON (UPI) - Prime Minister Margaret Thatcher
repeatedly declined to answer questions in
Parliament Tuesday about a reported rift between
her and Queen Elizabeth that raised fears of a
British constitutional crisis.
        The growing political controversy that
enveloped the traditionally neutral Buckingham
Palace threatened to add a sour note to Wednes-
day's royal wedding of Prince Andrew and Sarah
Ferguson.
        On the eve of the wedding, Thatcher was
repeatedly asked during her regular question-and-
answer session in the House of Commons about her
relationship with Queen Elizabeth II.
        "I intend to follow the well established
policy of my predecessors and not answer
questions directly or indirectly about the
monarch," Thatcher replied each time.
        The heated questions stemmed from an
article in The Sunday Times that cited sources
close to the queen as saying Queen Elizabeth
considered Thatcher's policies "often to be
uncaring, confrontational and socially divisive."
        The Royal Family is supposed to remain
neutral politically.
        The queen's press secretary, Michael Shea,
vehemently denied The Sunday Times story. But
editor Andrew Neil responded by disclosing that
the sources for the story were "within the
palace" and had volunteered the information.
```

Reprinted with permission of United Press International, Copyright 1986.

Figure 3.3 — Thatcher: ELECTRA Version

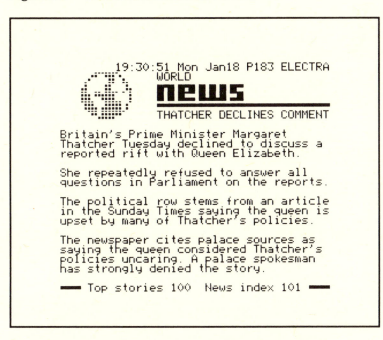

Used with permission of Great American Broadcasting.

As you will probably have discovered, saving one character can make the difference between a story that will fit and one that won't (see Figure 3.3 for the ELECTRA version). There are a few things you can look out for when trying to save space on a page:

1. Paragraphs that have a very short last line can often be rewritten to save that line.
2. Long paragraphs have more scope for editing than short ones. You can nearly always simplify a paragraph of five lines or more, and the text will probably benefit from the pruning.
3. Long words can often be replaced by shorter ones. Some words are dear to the videotex editor's heart. In a tight corner, reduction can become cut; negotiations — talks; following — after; decline — dip, drop, slip, slump; victory — win.

4. Sometimes using two short words instead of one long one can enable you to fit what you need to say into the available space: "Parkersburg council members have turneddown..." (39 + 4 characters) fits better than "Parkersburg council members have rejected..." (32 + 8 characters). But there are occasions when using one long word instead of two short ones can save space. For instance, "Newport council members have rejected..." (37 characters) fits on one line, whereas "Newport council members have turned down..." (40 characters) does not.

5. Reported speech can save you a great deal of space and gives you the liberty to do some editing. It usually reads better on the screen, too.

6. Often you have to use the electronic editor's equivalent of the scalpel and discard some details from the story. Look for details that are not of direct importance. For instance, you can often leave out the names of attorneys from court reports: "John Smith's lawyer, Fred Jones, told the jury..." could easily read "John Smith's lawyer told the jury...."

There are some options you should not exercise in the name of saving space. Writers need to be aware of how the eye reads the text and thus avoid complicating the reading process. Avoid abbreviations. They seem an obvious way to save space but can turn a story into an unintelligible jumble of letters, such as:

Former Sen Jennings Randolph, D-W Va, will address the 36th KY AFP convention at the Hyatt hotel, 2nd St, Sat Aug 4.

Spell out names in full on first reference unless they are very common acronyms, such as NATO, CIA, FBI, AFL-CIO, and avoid clumps of acronyms that can get to sound like some strange code. The second sentence that follows reads better than the first:

The EPA has called in the FBI to investigate the dumping of PCBs.

The Environmental Protection Agency has called in the FBI to investigate the dumping of toxic chemicals.

You should not try to save space by abbreviating titles, street names, or state names as the eye ends up doing a double take on such mutilated words as Pres Reagan, KY Gov Martha Layne Collins, Commerce Dept, and Sec of State. For much the same reason, you should avoid using the ampersand or percent sign. It actually takes the eye longer to recognize the symbol "&" than to read the word "and" written out in full. When space is a problem, there is always a better way to make the text fit than resorting to abbreviation.

Hyphenation is not the answer to space problems, either. Some videotex operations have opted to use the newspaper technique of splitting words at the end of lines. Once again, the space saved by hyphenation scarcely seems worth the increased difficulty encountered in reading and understanding the text on the screen. Some services even leave half a word at the end of a page, no doubt espousing the newspaper lore that says people are more likely to turn to a story continuation if you leave them mid-word, mid-thought, mid-sentence. What sounds a reasonable proposition in a 1,000-word newspaper story becomes merely aggravating when used at 75-word intervals in a videotex report (see Figure 3.4).

Every videotex operation has its own peculiarities of style — many of them stemming from the idiosyncrasies of early editors. CEEFAX still cherishes a total ban on the term "gunned down" largely because of the aversion of its editor-in-chief, while ELECTRA doggedly insists that the Soviet news agency TASS is an acronym and therefore upper case no matter what UPI and the Associated Press say. Such rules exist to achieve uniformity among the various writers and avoid references to SALT II on one page and SALT-2 on another, protesters and protestors, TASS and Tass. Stylistic consistency helps both the writer and the reader, though writers do not always see it that way. "Some don't really think it's important. Some agree that basically there should be uniformity for reading ease if nothing else. Still others are prepared to duel over a wayward lowercase" (*AP Style Guide,* 1980).

Videotex style is meant for the eye rather than the ear, which is one of the reasons television and radio writers often have a hard time adapting to electronic text. When language gets too

Figure 3.4 — Gulf War Stories

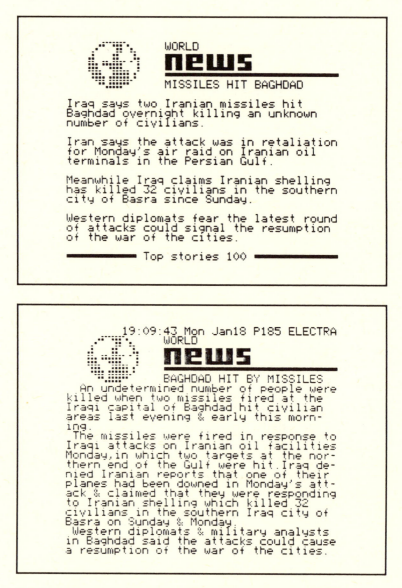

WORLD
news
MISSILES HIT BAGHDAD

Iraq says two Iranian missiles hit
Baghdad overnight killing an unknown
number of civilians.

Iran says the attack was in retaliation
for Monday's air raid on Iranian oil
terminals in the Persian Gulf.

Meanwhile Iraq claims Iranian shelling
has killed 32 civilians in the southern
city of Basra since Sunday.

Western diplomats fear the latest round
of attacks could signal the resumption
of the war of the cities.

━━━━━━━━ Top stories 100 ━━━━

19:09:43 Mon Jan18 P185 ELECTRA
WORLD
news
BAGHDAD HIT BY MISSILES
An undetermined number of people were
killed when two missiles fired at the
Iraqi capital of Baghdad hit civilian
areas last evening & early this morning.
The missiles were fired in response to
Iraqi attacks on Iranian oil facilities
Monday,in which two targets at the nor-
thern end of the Gulf were hit.Iraq de-
nied Iranian reports that one of their
planes had been downed in Monday's attack & claimed that they were responding
to Iranian shelling which killed 32
civilians in the southern Iraq city of
Basra on Sunday & Monday.
Western diplomats & military analysts
in Baghdad said the attacks could cause
a resumption of the war of the cities.

Used with permission of Great American Broadcasting.

informal, it looks uncomfortable on the screen. There is no place for people being "thrown in the slammer" or the dozens of slang equivalents that crop up daily in radio news broadcasts. Such contractions as don't, won't, isn't, you're, and they'll tend to disrupt the flow as the eye scans the page. You should only use such contractions in a direct quote or in very light pieces where more formal versions would look stilted.

Keep punctuation to a minimum. Pages festooned with commas, semicolons, quotation marks, dots, and dashes are distracting, and so it is usually better to be parsimonious with punctuation. Obviously, you need to retain punctuation marks that make the text easier to follow, but it makes sense to remove the periods after such abbreviations as Mr, Jr, Dr, and in acronyms such as US, FBI, and CIA. Pages littered with quotation marks also slow down the reader, and so you should omit inverted commas around the titles of books, plays, or movies. You can show you are referring to a title by capitalizing the main words:

John Le Carre based A Perfect Spy on his own experiences as an intelligence agent.

Or:

Bob Dylan's classic Like a Rolling Stone...

Often the newswires put small snippets of a speech into quotation marks. "The president said he was 'appalled' at the latest arms proposal." It is usually best to avoid the practice when using reported speech. If you want to use a quote, you should try to use enough of what was said to give a real flavor of the speech. Unless you have a great quote, it is better to use reported speech and paraphrase what has been said, keeping as close to the original as possible. If you do opt to use a direct quote, you must use the exact words.

Headlines are another important aspect of writing for videotex and teletext. There are two basic kinds of headlines — those on the top of pages that serve the same function as newspaper headlines and those on separate headline or index pages that are designed to prompt the reader to request a page. Headlines on the top of a story should always indicate the newest angle so readers can tell at a glance if the page has been updated since the last time they looked at it. Headline pages — sometimes called indexes or menus — help guide readers round an otherwise uncharted database. Both kinds of headlines should be short, catchy, but above all informative.

Headline writing is an art of its own. "The Perfect headline neatly encapsulates all the points of the story underneath. At the same time, it is snappy and so worded as to force you to read on. It doesn't, of course, exist" (Walker, 1985). Headlines present the same challenge to electronic editors as to those in newspapers and magazines. The general guidelines are the same for both:

1. Always emphasize the newest angle.
2. Headlines need a verb — and preferably one in the present tense and active voice. As desk editors are always told, "Man Bites Dog" is probably the perfect headline.
3. Keep punctuation to a minimum, and do not hyphenate words used in headlines of more than one line.
4. Acronyms, abbreviations, numerals, and colloquialisms come into their own here. Such words as nix, slam, rap, slate, and probe are fair game.
5. Accuracy is more important than any of the previous points. Opt for an uninspired label rather than be inaccurate.
6. Make sure your headline makes sense. After juggling around with words for a while, editors occasionally lose track of what they really want to say.
7. Check to be sure that your headline doesn't say something that you don't intend it to. "General flies back to front" conjures up a couple of very different pictures.

NOTES

1. The Modified FOG Index Formula used to calculate reading age is $[(A+P) \times 0.4] + 6$, where A is the average number of words per sentence, and P is the percentage of words with three or more syllables (Peter Winter).

4

THE ELECTRONIC
NEWSPAPER

Most videotex editors dread the inevitable cocktail party question, "And what do you do?" On such occasions, one takes a deep breath and boldly says, "I'm an editor on a teletext service," (blank stares) "...that's an electronic newspaper" (more blank stares) "...it's like a newspaper printed on your TV screen..." (look of partial comprehension or parting shot of "How nice"). A newspaper printed on your TV screen is the easiest way to explain the concept of electronic publishing to the person in the street — or in the TV store. Technical purists might prefer the term information retrieval service, but such a soulless epithet is unlikely to find favor with the writers and editors who produce the information or the readers who retrieve it. Each electronic newspaper has its own character, its own distinctive design, and stylistic quirks. It takes a great leap of faith to imagine anything distinctive or quirky about an information retrieval service.

Still, it would be wrong to assume that a teletext service or the information services on two-way videotex are nothing more than the morning newspaper entered into a database. Various information providers, both in the United States and Britain, have attempted to serve up copy straight from their typesetting computers and have found there is little value in the exercise. Compuserve found that once the initial novelty wore off, people did not really want to read their local newspaper from an electronic screen. An experiment in in the first part of 1982 provides some interesting figures. In February 1,200 of a total 5,882 accesses were of Compuserve electronic newspapers, compared to 136 of 6,681 accesses in June (*International Videotex and Teletext News,* 1982). It seems neither the content nor the form played to the strengths of the new medium. Much of the information lacked timeliness and was presented in a form that was never designed to be displayed on the electronic screen.

Videotex is balanced precariously between the traditional worlds of the print and broadcast media. Two-way videotex has closer links with publishing, while teletext tends to be the broadcasters' province. You can usually tell the background of those involved in a service by the terminology they use. Broadcasters talk of videotex programming, while publishers refer to content. Journalists talk of headlines and teases, computer systems people deal with menus and prompts, publishers use indexes and references.

Both teletext and videotex provide the immediacy of broadcasting along with the lasting power of the printed word. Both are more comfortable handling the headline-type news found on radio and TV, although they use many of the stylistic conventions of the newspaper story.

So far the Federal Communications Commission has favored the idea of teletext as a newspaper, affording electronic publishing First Amendment protection and relief from many of the restrictions that apply to broadcasters in its May 1983 Report and Order. As yet, the debate has been largely theoretical. No one has yet tried using teletext to report on matters that would be barred from TV screens. So far, no one has tried advertising liquor, cigarettes, or other items that could not be advertised on regular broadcast media. The first time someone tries to apply the fairness doctrine to a teletext service or uses electronic text to cover a story in a way that could not be broadcast by the TV station the signal of which carries the text service, then it will become clear whether teletext is truly deemed to be an electronic newspaper.

Both printed and electronic newspapers are dealing with the written word. Writers and editors are producing copy for the eye rather than the ear, which has major implications for style. Most videotex operations, either consciously or unconsciously, aim for a style that recreates the tone of a quality newspaper, although electronic text has to be more tightly written because of space and format limitations. Like its printed counterpart, videotex style aims to be simple but not colloquial.

In both media the text has to be easy to read and has to look good on the page. Both have to take into account the physical process of reading — the way the eye moves over the page and recognizes words. For example, psychologists have proved that the eye recognizes groups of letters, especially those with ascenders and descenders, rather than reading each letter individually. That is one of the reasons newspapers favor headlines in upper and lower case. Blocks of copy written completely in capitals — and thus without any ascenders or descenders — are much harder to read than copy written in upper and lower case. They look solid and intimidating whether printed on paper or on the electronic screen. These are the kinds of issues that are important for those working with both print and electronic text.

Newspaper page designers and electronic text editors are concerned with the final look of pages. Obviously, a newspaper page with five or six stories, a photograph, grey tints or reverse blocks, rules, and headlines is a much more complicated entity than the single-story videotex page. Nevertheless, the use of space or graphic devices, such as bullets and boxes, are equally important to the appeal and sense of movement of a videotex page. Sometimes the spaces between words can create a strong, and distracting, diagonal line across the screen. Such problems can be avoided by a minor rewrite. On slow days teletext editors on both sides of the Atlantic have been known to amuse themselves by trying to make all the lines on a page the same length. It is a practice that does more for the mental agility of the editor than the comprehension of any potential reader. Solid slabs of text, especially on index pages, are intimidating and difficult to read. Electronic text editors have to be able to spot the problem areas and use the visual strengths of their medium to help convey their message in a lively and effective way.

Both newspapers and electronic text services allow readers to absorb the information at their own pace. You choose what to read, when to read it, and pretty much in what order. If you have trouble understanding a sentence, you can always read it again, or refer back to a story later. The ability to refer back and forward carries its own responsibilities. Factual accuracy and stylistic consistency are vital to the credibility of both printed and electronic newspapers.

In both videotex and print, mistakes jump off the page at you, whereas TV and radio newscasters are on to the next story before anyone has really noticed a slipup. Every videotex operation has its horror stories about the typos that got away. The BBC has had its Irish Republican Army hootings (and shoutings) in Belfast, while ELECTRA once carried a story about a hearing on venereal disease, missing a vital *l* from the phrase "public inquiry." Happily videotex typos can be corrected the instant someone spots them — ideally before the page is broadcast or goes live on the database. Once committed to print, newspaper errors live on forever — and there seems to be some press-room gremlin that ensures that major misadventures occur in forty-eight-point bold. It could take a whole career to live down such a classic as "Incest more common than thought in US."

Desk editors know that of the cardinal sins, one of the worst is spelling someone's name two different ways in a story. Cynics suggest it is better to err consistently. Consistency of style is more than pure pedantry. If some stories refer to events in Peking and others to Beijing, the reader is likely to be confused into thinking these are two separate Chinese cities. If some writers spell canceled with one *l* and some cancelled with two, readers assume one of the variants is wrong — even though Webster's dictionary says both are acceptable. Stylistic inconsistencies make both printed and electronic newspapers look sloppy.

Printed information gives readers control over their reading. Although newspapers, magazines, and books are arranged in a linear manner with the pages following each other in a logical sequence, you can disregard that linearity and follow your own preferences. British newspapers work on the assumption that most Britons glance at the front page, then the back, before launching into the body of a newspaper. That could be symptomatic of the anarchic tendencies of the British or simply because most newspapers are read on crowded trains. Whatever the reason, few people begin at the beginning and proceed in an organized manner through a publication. They jump about, selecting items that look appealing.

Many teletext databases imitate the structure of newspapers or magazines. Pages are put together in such categories as news, weather, sports, business, and features in much the same way a newspaper is divided into sections. The pages are numbered sequentially, but the pages are not physically stored next to each other. If you have just finished reading a sports story on page 133, you can move on to another sports page (134) or the stock market report (page 147) or the news index (page 101) with equal ease and expect them to arrive on the screen with equal speed. Two-way videotex does not even try to suggest linearity. You have to access pages by a hierarchy of indexes or keywords.

USA Today is often referred to as a videotex newspaper. The emphasis on many short, highly edited stories could come straight from the electronic media's philosophy. *USA Today* revels in the use of color, tables, charts, and graphs in ways that could easily be translated to or from the electronic screen. Major stories are broken up in much the same way a videotex editor separates out the main angles of a story and presents them in a multipage sequence.

The tone of *USA Today* may be that of videotex, but it is still burdened by the slowness and expense of newspaper production. The rising costs of printing and distribution have led some pessimists to consider putting the newspaper on the endangered species list. Several hours go by between the final deadline when the newspaper is put to bed and its arrival on the front porch or the newsstand. The same news stories can distributed via videotex in a matter of minutes and without the cost of paper, ink, or delivery.

Radio and TV mean that newspapers have long since given up the idea of being first with the news. The Miami *Herald* broke the story that took Gary Hart out of the presidential campaign in April 1987 but only as a result of substantial investigative effort. Generally, it is rare that a newspaper gets to break a story. Videotex, on the other hand, outpaces everything except live TV and radio coverage of an event. From the moment the bulletin buzzer sounds, it takes less than a minute to air a newsflash and usually only a couple of minutes to write the first story. David Klein reviewed his experience with teletext while he was media critic with the Cincinnati *Post:*

> I had called up the latest news update on the TV set. This printed information appeared: "The Korean airline 747 carrying 267 people to Seoul has been missing since 2:23 p.m....The flight was expected at 4:30 p.m. eastern time." This was at 9:45 p.m.on a Wednesday night.... At that time, most Americans weren't even aware that a crisis was brewing. The next TV newscast was more than an hour away, and the next newspaper edition was many hours distant (Klein, 1983).

The updating process is so simple that both editorial and advertising departments can make changes much more easily and cheaply than on a newspaper. A supermarket could change its special offers every hour, and if it ran out of the featured hotdogs, it could switch the ad to offer ground beef. Such changes can be made with a phone call and on the air in little more than the time it takes to type the update. When a network changes the evening's TV schedule to air a presidential address, the teletext TV listings can be altered accordingly. The traditional newspaper could not hope to accommodate such changes.

Much of the success of a videotex service depends on its timeliness. Competition is at its keenest between rival teletext services. In Britain ORACLE and CEEFAX constantly monitor each other's newsflash page and are mightily miffed if the competition comes up with something they are not aware of. A matter of minutes can be important in teletext terms.

The only deadline in a videotex operation is "as soon as possible." There is no press time, no fixed cutoff point beyond which a story misses today's edition. The constant deadline produces fewer ulcers and sharp exchanges, but it does mean the pressure to produce is always present. There is nothing akin to the great sense of relief when a newspaper is put to bed, no slow buildup to the hectic hours before deadline. A videotex writer can always improve a story, always update something.

ELECTRA readers sometimes refer to teletext as "real time news." Teletext and two-way videotex can bring people news as it happens rather than serving it up at appointed times of the day. There is no need to bridge the interval between when a story is written and the time it will be read. The famous "Dewey Elected" headline would not have happened on videotex. Sometimes videotex editors can prepare ahead of time for certain news stories, but those occasions are the exception rather than the rule. Every time Pete Rose came up to bat in the later part of the 1985 season, ELECTRA was ready with a newsflash announcing his historic 4,192nd hit. About the same time Rose reached first base on September 11, 1985, the flash was on the air. But few stories can be predicted and prepared for quite as readily.

Instant updating brings its share of problems as well as advantages. Often videotex editors are faced with decisions that only confront newspaper editors as the final deadline approaches. Few newspaper editors have to cope with the kind of dilemma that became a part of everyday life at CEEFAX during the Falklands War. Do you report that the Argentine Navy is claiming to have sunk a British warship, when the Defense Ministry is refusing to confirm or deny the report? Even if you attribute the story and make clear the report is unconfirmed, are you justified in alarming everyone with relatives on the ship? Or do you ignore the story and risk being preempted by others? Instant news does not relieve editors of their responsibility to check the facts and avoid reporting mere rumor, but it can make that task very difficult.

The speed with which copy can be on the air can also create serious problems when the newswires decide to kill a piece. Soviet leader Leonid Brezhnev "died" several times on teletext before he was finally laid to rest on November 11, 1982. By the time the bulletin buzzer is sounding with a message to kill the offending story, it could well be on the air.

When big news breaks, newspaper editors set about remaking the front page, cutting stories, or relegating them to an inside page to accommodate the latest scoop. With teletext, that is a part of the routine. Throughout the day editors oust old stories to make way for new ones, making and remaking the news section and the sports and business sections. One of the hardest things for a newcomer to master is the art of updating — knowing what to replace and when to replace it. The content is constantly changing. In the average day a twenty-page news section may well have seen sixty stories come and go.

Newspapers have the space to carry the whole day's worth of teletext news — but in the next morning's edition. Newspapers and two-way videotex have the capacity to print much larger quantities of information than teletext. It could take most of an on-air teletext magazine to broadcast all the college sports scores that a newspaper crams into a couple of columns of six-point type.

Probably the most obvious difference between the two news media is in story length. A newspaper story can run 1,000 words, while an editor on a two-way videotex service may have a couple of hundred words to play with and a teletext editor 75. Videotex will always be more comfortable handling brief headline-type news. Newspapers have come to find their niche in analysis, background, investigation, and commentary. Their strength is in explaining what the news means and not just what has happened. As a result, most people look to newspapers for greater depth or insight into events rather than the latest details. People still turn to newspapers for the analysis of last night's baseball game even though they already know the score from the electronic media. They want to read the full details of the council debate on banning pitbulls rather than the brief snippets they saw on TV.

The luxury of length allows newspaper and magazine writers much more freedom to develop a story. Most newspaper stories tend to follow the basic pyramid structure. The story begins very focused and then broadens out. A twenty-to-forty-word lead encapsulates the main points, giving the who, what, when, where, and why of the story. The next few paragraphs fill out the story with a good quote or brief background information and an expansion of the points made in the lead. Then comes another layer including more detail and more background. The layered approach allows for easy editing. Should desk editors need to cut 200 words from the piece, they can safely lop them off the bottom of a well written story without sacrificing any point that is vital to the main thrust of the piece. Writers hope that the flow of their fine prose will carry readers through to the very last period, but the pyramid structure ensures that readers who opt out after a couple of paragraphs will still have gleaned the central points.

The pyramid structure is inappropriate for videotex writing, given that the average page can hold little more than a newspaper lead. There is no space to state and then expand on the themes. As one ELECTRA editor remarked "What you're dealing with here is more of a box than a pyramid." With a multiple-page story you are dealing with many boxes, each quite distinct in its theme, and each contributing to the overall picture. (Compare teletext, newspaper, radio, and TV versions of the same story in Figures 4.1 to 4.4.)

In the same way that a newspaper writer structures a story to emphasize the most important facts, newspaper editors and page designers use different type and headline sizes to indicate which are the most important stories. Positioning within the newspaper and on an individual page is an editorial value judgment. By their decision about what appears on the front page, or even what appears above the fold on the front page, editors are telling readers that these are stories they should not miss. Beyond the decision that a story warrants inclusion in the database, videotex editors leave decisions on relative importance to the reader. Each videotex reader decides what is important to himself or herself.

Videotex editors use indexes and teases to tell readers what is available but without implying the relative value of different pages. Readers cannot browse randomly through a database. They rarely stumble fortuitously across something that takes

Figure 4.1 — Teletext Story

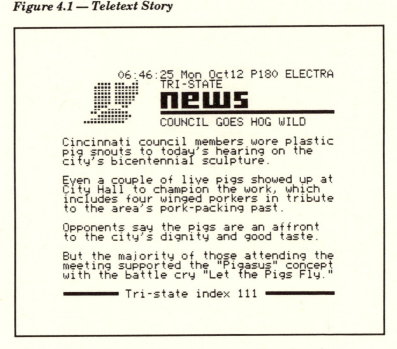

Used with permission of Great American Broadcasting.

their interest the way a newspaper or magazine reader does. Videotex readers purposefully summon the information they want to the screen. It is therefore very important for a videotex service to ensure that people know what is available and where to find it. Newspapers index general categories of information, such as weather or TV listings, but they do not index individual stories. They generally tease a couple of major pieces from the front page of each section, but they generally assume the reader will find what they want by glancing through the pages. Indeed, they aim to encourage such browsing for the sake of their advertisers.

Obviously, newspapers have the benefit of being able to use photographs to dramatize a story in a way only equaled by video

Figure 4.2 — Newspaper Story

Crowd roots for pigs
Few at hearing want sculpture butchered
By Christine Wolff

Tuesday was a grand day to be a pig in Cincinnati.

Pigs were praised, petted, displayed, and defended. Three city councilmen wore pig snouts on their heads.

And cuddly, pink-eared Arnold, a week-old piglet borrowed from a farm in Butler County for the occasion, sprouted paper wings.

For almost two hours Tuesday, the talk in city council chambers centered on pigs — pigs as art versus pigs as a nasty joke.

The outcome: Pigs are funny art, and the four controversial red-winged swines planned for atop the elaborate Sawyer Point Park sculpture are here to stay.

The pigs weren't in danger of toppling to negative opinion. The meeting, called to allow the public a say about the pigs, began with an opinion from council's attorney that council was powerless to change the sculpture.

The vocal majority of the crowd crammed into the council chambers and on the overhead balcony was decidedly pro-pig. A banner taped to the walls said, "Keep the Pigs — Throw the Bums Out."

About 15 students from the University of Cincinnati School of Fine Arts carried cardboard pigs on wooden sticks, with the message "Pro-Art" and "Let the Pigs Fly."

Milton Bortz sat in the midst of the outpouring of pig love and stoi-cally waited his turn to speak. He liked the sculpture, he said, but the winged pigs had to go.

"We could have Picassos and fine art statues all over that artwork and the focus would still be on those three-foot pigs," said Bortz, a cousin of pro-pig Councilman Arn Bortz, who sat across from him wearing a plastic pig snout and a pig-snout hat on his head.

Councilmen John Mirlisena and Peter Strauss joined Bortz in pig paraphernalia.

"This is not the right image for our city," Milton Bortz said. "You (the council) have the duty to protect us from scorn."

Miriam Bernstein agreed that the pigs are cute, then described what "Porkopolis" — Cincinnati's nickname in the 1880s — was actually like.

"We have fantasized the pigs. We think of a child's soft stuffed toy," she said. "But the children of the 1800s didn't see pigs that way. There were 500,000 pigs running through the streets of Cincinnati. They were a menace, a danger and rightfully were put in their place."

At Sawyer Point Park, on the riverbank at the foot of Eggleston Avenue, pilings are being driven to support the sprawling artwork. The 200-pound pigs are being readied for casting in Minneapolis.

Reprinted with permission of the Cincinnati Enquirer.

Figure 4.3 — Radio Story

```
CINCINNATI COUNCIL PIG FIGHT


        CINCINNATI HAS GONE HOG-WILD OVER PINK,
FLYING PIGS PLANNED FOR THE TOP OF A SAWYER
POINT STATUE.  LITERALLY HUNDREDS OF PEOPLE
SHOWED UP FOR A PUBLIC HEARING ON THE PORCELAIN
PORKERS AT CITY HALL TODAY:
CART (PRO_PIG SPOKESMAN)  ......OUR IMAGE.
(CHEERS FADE)" 14 SEC
MOST OF THE CROWD ECHOED HIS PRO-PIG STANCE.
IN FACT, THERE WAS GENUINE SURPRISE FROM THE
ANTI-PIG PEOPLE, WHO BELIEVED THAT ALL THEY
NEEDED TO DO WAS CHEW THE FAT AND THE PIGS WOULD
GO AWAY:
CART (ANTI-PIG SPOKESMAN)  ......SUCH SUP-
PORT."    12 SEC
IRONICALLY, EVEN THOUGH MORE PEOPLE SHOWED UP
AT THIS PUBLIC HEARING THAN AT ANY IN WELL OVER
A DECADE, COUNCIL WILL NEVER EVEN VOTE ON THE
ISSUE.
        IT'S UP TO THE BICENTENNIAL COMMISSION,
AND THEY ALREADY BELIEVE WHEN IT COMES TO ART,
THE PIGS PLAY A PART.
```

Used with permission of Don Jensen, WKRC Radio.

Figure 4.4a — TV Story

```
ON NICK KEY SS      THOSE WINGED PIGS THAT
                    ARE TO BE CAST IN BRONZE
                    TO FLY ABOVE THE COLUMNS
                    AT SAWYER POINT HAVE
                    BROUGHT ON A RAGING
                    DEBATE.
                    BICENTENNIAL PLANNERS
                    TRIED TODAY TO CONVINCE
                    RESIDENTS THAT A FLYING
                    PIG SCULPTURE WON'T
                    HARM THE QUEEN CITY'S
                    IMAGE...BUT STILL MANY
                    PEOPLE THINK THE
                    SCULPTURE'S HOGWASH..
CUT TO LANGFORD     EYEWITNESS 12'S
                    STEPHEN LANGFORD WAS
                    AT THE PUBLIC HEARING
                    TODAY..STEVE.....
                    (STEVE AD LIBS)
                    ROLLCUE:"

DISSOLVE LIVE REMOTE FULL AT :28
BACK ON LANGFORD/CHYRON: LIVE
```

Reprinted with permission from WKRC–TV.

Figure 4.4b — TV Story

```
ROLL CUE FOR PKG:
"TAKE VTR SOT UP FULL

OUT CUE: "a state of shock"
ON LANGFORD/LIVE
                    one hundred years ago these
                    little piggies went to
                    market

                    and earned cincinnati the
                    title of pork packing capi-
                    tal of the world.

                    british artist andrew
                    leicester found that out,
                    when he submitted this bid
                    to build the city's bicen-
                    tennial sculpture.

                    but his artistic conception
                    of cincinnati's history
                    provoked a political pigsty,

                    the mayor saying he wanted
                    no bicentennial barnyard.

                    such controversy is not new
                    to the artist...

                    leicester's work at a prison
                    in colorado, for example,

                    provoked state-wide scorn.

                    his sculpture of spitting
                    gargoyles, pregnant women,
                    and a man drowning, sent tax-
                    payers into a state of shock.
```

Reprinted with permission from WKRC–TV.

footage. Pictures play an even more vital role in news magazines. Some stories are even chosen on the strength of the photographs that go with them. News pictures heighten the drama of a story. A picture can show the anguish on the face of the parent of a missing child or the elation of a batter who has just scored the winning home run. Videotex editors have to rely on word pictures. Readers of an electronic newspaper do not get to see the mayor cut a ribbon on a new bridge or the president signing an arms treaty.

Newspapers have larger staffs than videotex or teletext operations. They are involved in the news-gathering business, as well as news dissemination. Almost all of those who work on newspapers are specialists — reporters, editors, artists, columnists, photographers. Teletext is largely a medium of editors and sometimes graphic artists. The same people select the news, write it, illustrate it if necessary, lay it out on the pages, index it, and proof it. A videotex story is a solo effort. The editor has almost total control of the whole process. There's no city editor, copy desk, layout artist, or proofreader to intervene — or catch any errors. Some operations divide up the responsibilities by category, with separate staffs to handle news, sports, and business. But such categories tend to be vague. On a busy Saturday at the BBC, the chief editor for news usually ends up typing in soccer scores with the best of them.

Many people suggest the advent of electronic newspapers presages the end of their traditional counterparts. As yet, there seems to be no cause for alarm. The newspaper will always fulfill different needs from the electronic newspaper. People enjoy browsing through the pages of a local daily, knowing at a glance what is in today's edition, following or ignoring the editors' priorities. The newspaper is portable; as yet, only science-fiction movies foresee the day when we will all walk around with our own personal TV screens. Putting aside the logistics, people will still read newspapers and news magazines for the same reason they do now. They offer something different — in-depth articles, the op-ed pages, the cartoons. Assuming one spends just ten minutes each day glancing through a newspaper, those same ten minutes at off-peak connection charges for an on-line database are likely to cost around two dollars. That is not one of world's great bargains when a printed newspaper costs thirty-five cents. Teletext, of course, is free but can include a much smaller quantity of information than a newspaper.

As a news source, videotex is the intellectual equivalent of grazing. You sit down to many small dishes rather than the more traditional four-course fare of the New York *Times.* Neither approach is intrinsically better than the other — they are simply different. Teletext and two-way videotex are attractive supplements rather than replacements for newspapers. The electronic newspaper offers rapid access to the most up-to-date information. It can satisfy specific information needs very quickly and efficiently. Printers mean stories and advertisements can be stored in hard copy form almost as easily as they can be clipped from a newspaper. But it seems unlikely that electronic databases — no matter how slick, sophisticated, and user friendly — will ever totally replace the printed newspaper. It is hard to imagine settling down to breakfast with an electronic screen. There will always be a place for the Washington *Post,* the Cincinnati *Enquirer* and the Bloom County *Picayune.*

5

TV NEWSPAPER OR PRINTED RADIO?

Someone at CEEFAX once came up with the term "printed radio" to describe the operational realities of teletext. Despite the fact that videotex uses print like newspapers and appears on a television screen, its overall news philosophy comes closest to radio. Radio journalists may have trouble getting to grips with written style, but they understand the process of handling the news for electronic publishing better than most.

Immediacy is the great asset of both radio and videotex. Drive-time newscasts are so frequent that they practically amount to the constant deadline of videotex. Radio newscasters and videotex editors can easily see the similarities in the stories they write and the daily routine. Writers for both media are constantly updating the news, constantly rewriting, refreshing, and reevaluating their stories. UPI describes its broadcast newswire as "a river of information in ever changing form" (*UPI Broadcast Style Book,* 1979). It is a description that fits videotex perfectly.

In television, however, the whole production process is geared toward that crucial half hour on the air. The news is written and delivered just once rather than the continuous process of videotex and radio. Both radio and TV newscasts have to be on the air at a certain time. However, a story that misses one radio deadline can be on the air in the next newscast, which is rarely more than an hour away. A TV story might have to wait until the next day. Videotex writers know none of the tyranny of the deadline. They have only self-generated pressure to produce the fastest, most accurate story possible — and, of course, the journalist's instinct to blow all competitors out of the water.

Both radio newscasters and videotex editors constantly make the same kind of decisions — when to use a story, when to update it, refresh it, or ditch it. In both fields there is great emphasis on speed, with videotex usually ahead by a nose. As former Taft Broadcasting vice-president Terry Connelly has told countless teletext gatherings, the only faster way to get news is to have a newswire in your home.

Videotex and radio have programming flexibility. Two-way videotex and teletext can easily add extra pages to cover a big event, while radio newscasts often go over their allotted five minutes. It is relatively simple for a radio station to go live, be it for a news conference by the local pro football team or a speech from the White House. TV with its fixed deadlines cannot hope to rival either videotex or radio in the speed stakes, nor does it have the same degree of programming flexibility. It takes an event of the magnitude of the shuttle disaster or the signing of a superpower arms treaty to justify preempting the daily soaps.

Radio and videotex newsrooms both operate with a skeleton crew compared to TV or newspapers. Their news operations are much less complex — and less costly — undertakings than their TV counterparts. Walk into the average videotex newsroom, and you will see a handful of journalists mulling over wire copy or typing at terminals. Even during drive time, a radio station will have just three or four reporters and anchors on hand. The cast of thousands is all a taped illusion. Callers to the ELECTRA teletext newsroom are always surprised to discover that six writers keep the service going eighteen hours a day, seven days a week. CEEFAX operates teletext services on two networks and regular cabletext scrolls with a staff of around twenty. Small staffs mean that specialization is an uncommon luxury. Videotex writers are expected to handle almost all aspects of the operation. The people who select the stories usually write them, illustrate them, index them, and proofread them. They generally answer the phones and make the coffee, too. In elaborate videotex news operations, a chief editor will decide what stories will be used, assignpage numbers, and then give them to an editor to write. Two-way videotex services sometimes have artists on hand to create graphics and usually employ production staff to manage the actual database, taking care of such things as page links and customer billing. In most cases, however, the videotex editor, like the radio anchor, has complete responsibility for his or her own work.

A TV newsroom has dozens of people doing many different specialized jobs. Reporters, writers, videographers, technicians, producers, graphic artists, and on-air talent all work together to produce thirty minutes or an hour of news show. Because of the complexities of the news operation, people work on small parts of the overall production. A reporter will cover one story each day, writers are concerned with just the links and the brief "tell" stories read by the anchor, while the producer coordinates the segments and decides what order they will run in.

In radio the only real distinction is between between news gathering and news presentation — between reporters who go out on the streets and anchors who do not — and that distinction is often blurred. Videotex newsrooms do not even have that distinction. Writers are rarely called on to leave the comfort of their computer terminals. Instead, they rely on newswires and other media reporters to do the news gathering. Videotex is not a reporter's medium. Indeed, on occasions when videotex journalists do sally forth, notebook in hands, they inevitably return with enough material for a full-length magazine piece and then anguish for hours over how to boil it down to 300 words.

Videotex is not live in the sense that radio and TV newscasts are. People often ask whether the words appear on the air as you type them. Happily for those who think faster than they type, pages do not go "live" until you transmit them. You get the chance to weigh your words and look for typos before exposing them to the rest of the world. In a sense, that is like radio and TV reports that are taped ahead of time. Videotex writers are spared the full potential for disaster in a live newscast. They do not have to extricate themselves from situations when a tape fails to run on cue or keep their cool when the expected tape of Soviet leader Gorbachev arriving in the United States turns out to be the Bonanza theme.

The pace and overall approach of radio and videotex operations are surprisingly similar. It is not coincidental that one of the main sources of information for CEEFAX is the BBC's own General News Service bureau, which primarily services the corporation's many radio newsrooms. ELECTRA uses a combined newspaper/broadcast wire from UPI for national and world news. A teletext service needs the longer stories found on the newspaper wire, as well as the sense of immediacy and movement found on the broadcast wire. The dual personality of videotex news becomes obvious if either type of copy becomes unavailable. For local information ELECTRA depends largely on the WKRC-TV and radio reporters. Radio news is generally more current and easier to adapt to the teletext format than TV scripts. Radio and videotex are both in their element dealing with a running story. They share the need to keep stories turning over throughout the day.

All three media are at their best handling headline news. None is well placed to give the kind of in-depth analysis of events found in the daily newspaper. In videotex it is usually a matter of space, while TV and radio have a hard time holding the attention of the audience through long and complex arguments. For different reasons brevity is important to all three media.

Writers in both videotex and radio newsrooms spend their days creating word pictures. Their main concern is trying to make their language vivid enough to tell the whole story in around one hundred words or thirty seconds. They have to be skilled in the art of compression, for unlike their TV colleagues, they do not have video to help out in the story-telling process.

TV writers are often describing events you can see happening on the accompanying videotape. They have to write around the visuals, making sure their words complement the images on the screen rather than stating the blatantly obvious. It is clearly redundant to point out that it is crowded, when the viewer can see that the streets are packed for the annual Riverfest. On the other hand, video can fill in some vital information gaps. Given that a portion of the populace thinks contra aid is a new kind of soft drink, file footage of the Nicaraguan rebels can save a lot of words when it comes to describing a debate on U.S. policy in Central America.

Videotex copy is written for the eye — radio and TV for the ear. Radio and TV style tries to approximate the rhythms and vocabulary of everyday speech. The spoken vocabulary is much smaller, while the conversational style calls for contractions — don't, won't can't, isn't — using the more formal versions for emphasis only. Contractions and colloquialisms sound natural but look unnatural when written and consequently are used sparingly in videotex. In broadcast style the words have to sound right, whereas electronic text has to look right. Spelling is rarely the strong suit of the broadcast writer, though names like Tegucigalpa come tripping off their tongues with ease. Broadcast writers spell phonetically and punctuate to aid delivery rather than according to the rules of grammar. Dashes and ellipses are the staple of broadcast copy, along with such marvels as the military "koo." Radio and TV scripts do not scorn sentences without verbs, or grammatical constructions that would make the average English teacher blanch. Any videotex editor who favors verbless sentences should probably be looking for a new job.

The permanence of the printed word puts a premium on accuracy of both facts and language. Poor spelling and grammar not only look bad but also harm the credibility of any videotex venture. Videotex writers have to proofread carefully for both typos and meaning. An ungrammatical sentence in a TV or radio newscast has gone by long before anyone has a chance to reach for their Fowler's *English Usage*. Videotex errors live on to accuse their perpetrators.

Videotex writers stand or fall by their words alone. Words and simple graphics are the only tools they have to hold the reader's attention or suggest various shades of meaning. Newscasting, on the other hand, is a performing art, with delivery a vital part of the news process. Bad delivery can distract listeners or viewers so much that they are unaware of the content, while good delivery can gloss over some of the shortcomings of a poor script. Newscasters can use their voices to help with comprehension. A change in tone or facial expression says that this piece of news is serious or lighthearted. A stern look might accompany a story about embezzlement allegations, while a relaxed smile prepares you for a story on a child recovering from a heart transplant. A good newscaster will even help the audience understand the story by emphasizing key words and ideas.

Videotex writers are aiming to impart information. Electronic text revels in facts, figures, maps, tables —but it cannot effectively create mood or atmosphere. Videotex can tell you what happened and even what it means, but it cannot put you on the scene. Sound actuality is the keystone of a radio newscast precisely because it can create mood. A broadcast writer could always paraphrase the words of a witness to a bank robbery in the same way that a videotex writer would. To do so would take less time and fewer words, but the witness's own words have much greater impact. The comments of a Wall Street analyst lend more credibility to a report on the stock market than those same words spoken by the newscaster.

Video is the most powerful part of a TV newscast. The images make you feel as though you were on the scene of a demonstration, a hostage standoff, or a daring rescue. TV can appeal to the emotions even more effectively than radio. Indeed, many people admit to reaching for a Kleenex when they saw toddler Jessica McLure pulled out of the well where she'd been trapped for three days. Videotex sticks with the plain facts. A teletext story on a demonstration might read: "Some 500 demonstrators are marching on City Hall to protest plans to close a shelter for the homeless. Police scuffled with several banner-waving marchers, but no one was arrested." TV would show the crowds, the banners, and the scuffles in glorious closeup. After reading the teletext report you would probably know as much about the protest and what, if any, action would be taken on the shelter, but you would not have seen the conflict or vicariously experienced the drama.

Movement and drama are key ingredients in a TV newscast and video helps capture both. It is sometimes suggested that local TV producers only feature a fire story if the photographer shot video of flames. Without flames, the piece would be consigned to a passing mention in videotex-type style. "Early this morning a fire destroyed a home in Glendale. No one was hurt. Fire officials estimate damage at $75,000." With flames, the piece could be a local lead on a slow weekend. Videotex is an intellectual medium without the sound and fury of either TV or radio. It offers news with immediacy but without an appeal to the emotions. Stories are chosen solely on their news content and presented more directly. Videotex writers do not have to write around sound or video. They do not have to introduce a piece of tape, play the tape, and then sum up the main points again. Repetition and recapitulation are essential to comprehension in broadcast news but have no place in videotex.

Its printed form gives videotex a major advantage over TV and radio. Information is available when you want it and for as long as you want it. There's no need to scramble for a pencil to write down the winning lottery numbers or a vital phone number. You can linger over the election results or racetrack winners as long as you want. Broadcast announcers know they have only one chance to get their message across. Viewers or listeners do not have the option of reading over a sentence again if it did not make sense the first time around. They cannot refer back to a previous story if they missed some crucial information. Videotex journalists hope their writing style is clear enough that the reader does not have to refer back, but the option is always there.

Radio is a very convenient medium. You can listen as you drive to work or go jogging. You can even take a radio into the shower. But convenience is a double-edged sword. Both radio and TV suffer from the problem that people are usually doing something else while listening or watching. They are shaving or getting dressed or sitting down to dinner, while the newscaster is doing his or her best to capture their attention. Teletext and two-way videotex have the advantage of the reader's undivided attention. Someone has actually gone to the trouble of keying in a page number and wants the information on that page. Videotex readers are active rather than the passive audience for TV and radio. Retrieving information from a database is as much a transaction as asking for one's bank balance. In both cases it is unwise to trifle with readers or waste their time. Videotex pages should be brief and to the point.

Videotex readers can absorb the information at their own rate, allowing editors to present more complex information. For instance, broadcast writers use figures sparingly and round off those they do use for fear of overburdening the audience with a mass of statistics. Because videotex information remains on your screen until you request another page, editors can effectively present even detailed financial information. They can further enhance the clarity of such statistics by using simple charts, graphs, or tables. Videotex can readily present more complex concepts than radio or TV because people take in more of what they read than what they hear. However, reading takes more effort, which means videotex journalists have to make the process as simple and painless as possible or risk their readers giving up on a story that involves too much work.

Back in 1935 Hadley Cantril and Gordon Allport wrote: "Not only is the radio easy to listen to, it is likewise more personal than the printed word. A voice belongs to a living person and living people arrest our attention and sustain our interest better than do printed words" (Cantril and Allport, 1971). They were comparing radio and newspapers, but their comments apply equally to a comparison of radio and videotex or television and videotex.

Broadcast announcers aim to make each listener feel as though he or she is being addressed individually while videotex opts for a more impersonal style. In the words of one Cincinnati newscaster, "radio listeners must be 'you-ed' to death" in the effort to grab their attention. Broadcast writers go to great lengths to point out the relevance of each story to the lives of their audience. "You can expect to pay higher phone bills from next month...." could be the opening line of a broadcast story the videotex version of which might read, "The government has approved AT&T's call for phone access charges. Consumers can expect to pay higher phone bills from next month."

Radio and TV communication is person to person, with the personality of the reporter or newscaster an important part of the equation. Viewers relate very closely to TV anchors. They watch Peter Jennings or Dan Rather or Tom Brokaw rather than the news on ABC, CBS, or NBC. Strong personalities can carry a TV newscast, whereas videotex is judged on the quality of its information.

News anchors and reporters must develop their own personal style of delivery, while videotex writers must take their tone from the overall content and presentation of the service. A sports service would use a different style and layout from a business service, but within each service writers aim for stylistic conformity rather than individuality. After working with a group of writers for a while, it is always possible to spot subtle differences in story selection and style, but from the outside a service should appear truly "seamless," to use a word adopted by Time Inc.'s teletext team.

Radio and TV often find themselves embroiled in the debate about their own role. Should they try to entertain or inform or do both? As Herbert Gans notes, "Journalists' unending effort to achieve clarity exists mainly to minimize the audience's burden and their belief that the audience must not be burdened reflects their awareness that they are sometimes imposing an unwanted product" (Gans, 1980). Videotex does not impose an unwanted product. Videotex readers have control over what they read and when they read it. Videotex writers do not have to appeal to all the people all the time. Different pages and sections satisfy different needs. People who just want baseball scores can access them without sitting through twenty-five minutes of news. As a videotex editor, you are presenting business information to someone who has called up a stock market report. Your aim is to give the information as clearly as possible with no need for the drama of a multicolored bar chart that grows and rotates as you go into a commercial break. Readers who want entertainment can turn to the horoscope or computer games, or they can even go daydreaming through pages of vacation advertisements. It is all on offer all the time.

Broadcast news shows occur at specific times. They are complete and carefully orchestrated entities. The show begins at

the beginning and proceeds in orderly fashion toward its conclusion. A good show flows from one item to the next, including
suitable changes of tone and pace. The placement of the stories
is an important editorial decision. The newscast aims to grab
your attention early and hold onto it while the anchor leads you
through the day's events. TV and radio take their audiences on
a brisk guided tour, while videotex readers go at their own pace
and take their own route. The less structured approach means
that videotex editors have to provide adequate signposts to help
readers find their way to a story on the superpower summit or
the movie reviews. TV and radio newscasts use teases to tell you
what's coming up in the hope of dissuading you from pressing
buttons. Videotex teases and indexes are aimed at making you
start pressing those keys.

The scrolling pages of a cabletext service are, in effect, a
printed radio newscast. The scroll of pages does not allow
readers to control the proceedings, and so they become the
passive audience of radio and TV rather than taking the active
role of the videotex reader. The linear format of cabletext
presents the same kinds of problems for the editor as for a
broadcast writer, demanding stories that are as simple in their
structure as a radio piece. Generally, the pages contain less
information and more graphics than a teletext or two-way
videotex page. A cabletext scroll has to be orchestrated in much
the same way as a radio newscast, incorporating changes of tone
and pace to give the reader an occasional breathing space. Chief
editors at the BBC are sometimes called on to come up with
scrolls that fit very precisely in a five-minute time slot. It is a
task that comes as close to putting together a printed newscast
as anything in the business.

Inevitably, people ask whether videotex will harm TV and
radio. Videotex complements rather than competes with traditional media. A radio is much more portable than a TV screen.
It offers an easy way of catching up on the news without the effort
involved in videotex. TV has little to fear because people will
always want to see events happening and not just read about
them. Videotex simply offers another choice.

Live TV and radio coverage of an event will always edge out
videotex when it comes to speed and emotional impact, but

videotex can offer background information that makes those broadcasts meaningful to anyone who starts watching or listening part way through. During the congressional hearings on the Iran-contra scandal, ELECTRA carried summaries of what had been said so far in a session to help out those who had not spent the morning glued to their TVs. When the Challenger exploded, viewers who turned on their TV sets and discovered experts speculating on the future of the space program could instantly find out what had happened from teletext and thus make sense of the broadcast. Those without teletext had to wait until someone went back over what happened or showed the horrific footage of the explosion.

Usually, a teletext operation starts out under the aegis of a television news department with which it has little in common. Its style, its pace, its aims, and presentation are totally different. But the two services share the same TV screen — indeed, they are transmitted as one signal — and so are tied inextricably together. Because teletext hitches a ride on the video signal, it makes sense for the two types of news operation to exist side by side — if only to share news sources and engineering support. But such coexistence is not always peaceful and does not mean that either side has any great appreciation for the other's craft. Many of those in the TV news business have been resistant to what they see as a cuckoo in their nest waiting to steal viewers and ratings points. But actually, the two are so different they help each other.

In Britain, where teletext-equipped TVs are common, television commercials are often tagged to advertisements on teletext. A frame at the end of a commercial says, "For more information see ORACLE page 350." The fourth network's teletext service, 4-Tel, is devoted to program-related information. For instance, U.S. football is experiencing a boom in Britain, despite a serious shortage of information on the sport. The teletext service has stepped in to enlighten neophytes with explanations of plays, the rules, and biographical snippets to go along with the games that are televised on Channel 4. No better medium exists for TV listings, and teletext pages make effective teases for upcoming shows. A prompt on a teletext news page might read, "Ted

Koppel talks to George Bush on Nightline —11:30 pm on Channel 12."

No one expects readers to spend seven hours a day with a videotex service. Unlike TV or radio, videotex is a quick reference tool, a quick fix for the news junkie, a way to fulfill specific information needs or transactions. You don't settle down in front of the screen for a good read — ten to twenty minutes a day is about average. You want the main news stories or the sports scores or your bank balance with the minimum amount of fuss, and then you'll probably want to watch Nightline.

6

VISUAL DESIGN FOR ELECTRONIC TEXT

Most computer displays are designed to present information in linear form, like a research report or text. With advances in computer graphics, the computer display has become a pictorial medium capable of communicating information with visual immediacy, like a magazine or television advertisement. Knowledge of advertising design principles can help writers maximize the the communicative efficiency of their frames of text.

In advertising the purposeful arrangement of visual elements helps to convey specific messages. A frame of information displayed on a computer screen also attempts to convey specific messages, and the viewer can benefit from such advertising attributes as simplicity, clarity, order, and emphasis.

Although advertisements are intended to persuade and electronic text, for the most part, to inform, they can both use the same design method. Design decisions should be made for the purpose of reading efficiency, not for the writer's convenience. A false economy that squeezes too much information onto a single frame defeats the writer's purpose. The arrangement of visual information in an advertisement is ordered, not random. A page of electronic text should be ordered as well.

Many noteworthy texts discuss theories of design in both fine and commercial art. Arnheim (1954) and Dondis (1973) are good examples. But a succinct and easily understandable account of basic principles of graphic design is needed to assist electronic text writers in applying advertising design principles to the construction of computer frames. From the literature on advertising design, Roy Hall Nelson's book on design and layout, *The Design of Advertising* (1981), presents a distillation of design theory that the layperson can easily understand and use. Some concepts mentioned in Nelson's book that apply easily to computer programming form the structure of the first part of this chapter.

PRINCIPLES OF ADVERTISING DESIGN

Nelson describes five basic principles of design: balance, proportion, sequence, unity, and emphasis. Balance can be defined as the distribution of optical weight in a picture. Optical weight refers to the perception that some objects appear heavier than others. A balanced picture is one in which half of the weight is roughly on one side of the picture and half is on the other (see Figure 6.1). To achieve balance, the artist who designed the advertisement in Figure 6.1 arranged the dark-colored watchbands on the right side of the picture and the light-colored watchbands plus the text on the left side. Brown is visually heavier than silver, but the addition of the black print balances the visual weight of the picture.

Balance should not be confused with symmetry, in which the identical pattern occurs on both sides of the picture. A balanced frame creates feelings of stability and confidence in a viewer, while an unbalanced frame creates a feeling of stress. In some instances one might *want* to create a feeling of stress (with computer games, for example), but for the most part balance is to be preferred.

Figure 6.1 — Print Ad

Matched. Matchless. Seiko Lassale.
Design that reaches the realm of art.
Thinness at times almost two-dimensional,
born of highest quartz technology.

Other models available in 14K and 18K gold.

SEIKO
LASSALE

Reprinted with permission from Time Corporation.

A designer can control some elements of composition to achieve balance. For instance, color is visually heavier than black and white; big things are visually heavier than little things; black is visually heavier than white; irregular shapes are visually heavier than regular shapes. By controlling the color, size, tone, and shape of objects in a design, one distributes the visual weight and thus influences balance.

Proportion is the comparative relationship of the dimensions of objects to one another and their location in space vis-à-vis one another. These relationships involve height, width, depth, amount of surrounding space, degree of shading, and the intensity and choice of color. A well proportioned arrangement of objects contributes to the visual interest of a design. Good proportion is generally achieved by trying several alternative arrangements. The Greeks developed a guideline for determining good proportion in the physical dimensions of objects. This was expressed as a ratio called the "golden mean." It is arrived at by bisecting the square and using the diagonal of one half of the square as a radius to extend the dimensions of the square to become a "golden rectangle" (Dondis, 1973). Applied to a visual image, the golden mean translates into a rule of thirds, which asserts that significant objects are best distributed and arranged among the various thirds of a picture rather than in the center. In Figure 6.1 the picture is roughly divided into thirds, with watches in the top and middle thirds and text in the bottom third.

Sequence in design refers to the arrangement of objects in a picture in a way that facilitates the movement of the eye through the information displayed. In Figure 6.1 the eye moves from the gold watch faces in the upper left, down the silver watchbands to the gold faces of the watches in the middle third, then down the brown alligator-skin watchbands to the text, then down to the product name, and finally up the slightly textured bottom watchband and out of the advertisement. Normally, the eye, trained by reading, starts from the upper left (in this culture) and moves back and forth across the frame to the lower right. Perceptual psychologists have found that certain things attract the eye. It moves from big objects to small objects, from bright colors to subdued colors, from color to black and white, from irregular shapes to regular shapes, and from moving objects to still objects (Taylor, 1960). By manipulating eye attractors, a writer can plan how information in a frame will be ordered for use.

The principle of **unity** demands that the elements of a design look as if they belong together and that objects be related in size, shape, texture, and color. This does not mean that things should look identical, but they should be of the same order or category. For instance, the lettering in a frame need not be the same size but ought to be of the same style. Harmonious colors rather than clashing colors should be employed.

In addition to techniques for unifying the components of a picture, there are techniques for unifying the picture as a whole. Borders help the frame look unified, as does the use of an axis. Items in a design can be arranged to move out from the center of the axis. Lighter elements should be placed farther from the vehicle axis and larger elements should be placed closer to it. The final element, white space, can be manipulated to add unity. Several things grouped together and surrounded by white space will appear to belong together. In Figure 6.1 the display of watches is set apart by the border placed around them. However, the consumer is not to ignore the text, so to create dimensionality the artist moved the watches slightly back, allowing the text to advance toward the reader.

Emphasis is another important design principle. In an advertisement the most important object is emphasized, and the viewer's eye should go to it first. Advertisers have learned that when many objects vie for attention, confusion results and an ad may be ignored. Competition for attention is a problem in current computer-screen design. User discomfort, irritability, and inefficiency can result when an operator must continuously read confusing frames (Markower, 1981). An advertisement is planned so that the viewer's eye will automatically move to the area of emphasis. To create this emphasis, designers can use spot color; that is, they can put the brightest color in the most important place and use little additional color in the rest of the frame. The advertisement in Figure 6.1 appeared in *Forbes,* a business magazine for rising executives. The elegance of the watches was the point to be emphasized, so the gold of the watch faces serves as an eye attractor. The silver and the brown alligator skin of the watchbands reinforce the message of elegance.

The eye attractors mentioned earlier in connection with the sequence principle can also be used to add emphasis to objects in a frame. High contrast can be used to add emphasis and to make things stand out. Increasing the amount of white space surrounding an object sets it apart and makes it noticeable. Finally, light colors on a dark background appear to advance toward the viewer; dark colors on a light background appear to recede.

HUMAN FACTORS

Balance, proportion, sequence, unity, and emphasis are principles of graphic art theory developed to improve the effectiveness of visual communication. Another available body of knowledge about the organization of visual information specifically developed to improve human/computer interaction is human factors research. Graphic art theory prescribes what to do to get a certain positive effect; human factors research tells what not to do to avoid certain adverse effects. Human factors research often contains very detailed hard data; graphic art theory allows for the creative intuition of the artist. Graphic arts, on the whole, says more about pictorial information; human factors research, on the whole, says more about textual entities. Both the human factors scientist and the graphic artist must avoid information overload, unclear or irrelevant information, and user boredom or disinterest. In order to accomplish their tasks, human factors scientists draw knowledge from the fields of psychology and engineering, and graphic artists draw knowledge from fine arts theory and practice, Now, because of the advances in computer technology, the results of both lines of inquiry overlap and similarities emerge.

In a review of user considerations relating to software design of computer-based information systems, Williges and Williges (1981) compiled various dialogue design considerations that exist in the human factors literature specific to structuring information on visual display in an interactive environment. A comparison of those human/ computer dialogue design considerations with principles of graphic design illustrates that both human factors research and graphic art theory are concerned with the same basic principles and deal with them in complementary ways. Here is a comparison to human factors research that corresponds to the principles of balance, proportion, sequence, unity, and emphasis previously described.

Proportion

Proportion is the relationship of the dimensions of objects to one another and their location vis-à-vis one another.

Dialogue design considerations (Williges and Williges, 1981) that are consistent with the principle of proportion include the following:

Logically related data should be clearly grouped and separated from other categories of data. On large, uncluttered screens the display of functional areas should be separated by blank spaces (three to five rows and/or columns). On small and/or more cluttered screens structure can be defined by other coding techniques, such as using different surrounding line types, line widths, intensity levels, geometric shapes, color, and so forth (Engel and Granda, 1975; Galitz, 1981; Tullis, 1981).

Tabular displays should be broken into blocks, whenever possible. Breaking tabular displays into blocks improves search time (Cropper and Cropper, 1961; Ramsey and Atwood, 1979).

To avoid clutter, data should be presented using spacing, grouping, and columns to produce an orderly and legible display (Brown et al., 1981; Galitz, 1981).

In graphic applications attention should be given to the perception of area sizes depending on the foreground and surrounding colors. Warm colors, such as red and yellow, usually appear larger than cool colors, such as green and blue (Galitz, 1981; Miller, 1979; Tedford, Berquist, and Flynn, 1979).

Human factors researchers describe the importance of grouping and separating data by breaking them into blocks, using spacing, columns, borders, and by varying intensities and colors of groups of data.

Sequence

Sequence is the arrangement of objects in a way that facilitates the movement of the eye through a frame.

Dialogue design considerations (Williges and Williges, 1981) that are consistent with the principles of sequence include the following:

Information coding should be used to discriminate among different classes of items presented simultaneously on the display screen (Galitz, 1981; Miller and Thomas, 1976).

Color coding should be used to highlight related data that are spread about the display. Color coding may be used to locate headings, out-of-tolerance data, newly entered data, data requiring immediate attention, and to emphasize important data fields, differentiate groupings of data, and so forth (Brown et al., 1981; Galitz, 1981).

Data should be arranged on the screen so that the observation of similarities, differences, trends, and relationships is facilitated for the most common uses (Brown et al., 1981).

Displays should be designed so that information relevant to sequence control should be distinctive in position and/or format (Smith, 1981).

For data-entry dialogues, an obvious starting point in the upper-left corner of the screen should be provided (Parrish, et al., 1981).

For rapid scanning, lists should be left-justified and aligned vertically. Subclasses can be indented (Engel and Granda, 1975).

These research findings indicate that there should be a recognizable order to information displayed. The order can be created by using codes, highlighting, and by arranging items on the basis of similarities or relationships. Attention should be paid to starting points and to the progression of tasks. Further information, particularly lists, should be left-justified and vertically aligned.

Emphasis

Emphasis is the design of an object so that it catches the viewer's eye.

Dialogue design considerations (Williges and Williges, 1981) that are consistent with the principle of emphasis include the following:

To enhance important or infrequent messages and alarms, they should be placed in the central field of vision relative to the display window (Engel and Granda, 1975; Tullis, 1981).

Highlighting should be used for critical information, unusual values, items to be changed, items that have been changed, high-priority messages, the source of alarms, special function areas of the display, errors in entry, warnings of consequences of commands, and targets (Galitz, 1981; Parrish et al., 1981).

When an operation is to be performed on a single item in a display, the item should be highlighted (Engel and Granda, 1975).

Highlighting methods should be used to make prompts stand out (Brown et al., 1981).

On crowded displays, auxiliary codes, such as dim labels and bright data, should be used to distinguish the labels (Smith, 1981).

Instructions should stand out. For example, instructions may be preceded by a row of asterisks (Brown et al., 1981).

In graphics applications the cursor should be distinct from graphical shapes displayed. The cursor may also be differentiated by intensity, color, or blinking (Foley, Wallace, and Chan, 1981).

Maximum contrast should be maintained between scale markings and the value displayed (Bramack and Sinaiko, n.d.).

Unnecessary ornamentation, unwanted graphic patterns and illusions, and flaws in alignment should be avoided in graphic displays (Newman and Sproull, 1979).

Color should be used conservatively to avoid an appearance of clutter (Brown et al, 1981).

Information coding used to attract the user's attention should not be overused. Otherwise the value of such coding will be diminished and may become distracting (Galitz, 1981).

Only information essential to the user's current needs should be displayed (Brown et al., 1981).

The number of items displayed simultaneously should be minimized. As the number of displayed items increases, so does the time required by the user to detect and extract information that has changed. No more than 90 percent of the available character positions should be used (Brown et al., 1981; Coffey, 1961; Poulton and Brown, 1968; Ramsey and Atwood, 1979; Schutz, 1961; and Shields, 1980).

Human factors scientists have found that special visual treatment is necessary for critical information, such as high-priority messages, alarms, errors, prompts, and special instructions. Additionally, they have found that clutter should be avoided. Therefore, unnecessary ornamentation, over use of color, excessive coding, and the amount of information displayed should be limited.

Unity

In a unified design the objects look as if they belong together. They are related in size, shape, texture, and color.

Dialogue design considerations (Williges and Williges, 1981) that are consistent with the principle of unity include the following:

Data should be arranged in logical groups — sequentially, functionally, by importance, or by frequency (Brown et al., 1981).

Identical data should be presented to the user in a standard and consistent manner, despite its origin or module (Engel and Granda, 1975).

To convey separation, contrasting colors should be used. To convey similarity, similar but differentiable colors should be used (Galitz, 1981).

In graphic displays, the center of rotation should be the center of the object (Foley, Wallace, and Chan, 1981).

These research findings indicate that information must be presented to the user in a consistent and logical manner.

Balance

Balance is the distribution of optical weight in a picture so that half of the optical weight is roughly on one side of the picture and half is on the other.

The dialogue design considerations (Williges and Williges, 1981) that are consistent with the artistic principle of balance include the following:

Symmetrical balance should be maintained by centering titles and graphics (Galitz, 1981).

The unused areas should be used to separate logical groups, rather than having all the unused area on one side of the display (Brown et al., 1981).

Human factors scientists have found that balance is preferred in the display of titles, graphics, and in the arrangement of used and unused space.

Balance, proportion, sequence, unity, and emphasis are a good beginning for designers of computer displays. Their use will assist in establishing order in the arrangement of information and will increase the effectiveness of frame design.

Figure 6.2 is a frame produced at the University of Florida's Electronic Text Center for use on their cabletext system. The

Figure 6.2 — Electronic Ad

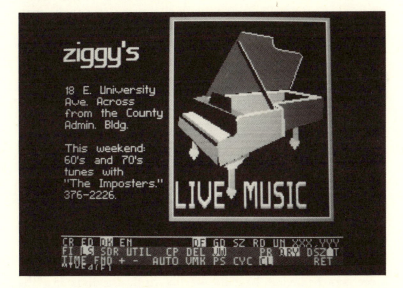

Copyright 1986. University of Florida, College of Journalism and Communications.

proportion adheres to the rule of thirds; the text occupies approximately one third of the space on the screen and the illustration, two thirds. The visual weight is distributed between the thirds, and the total effect is balanced. Although darker (heavier) shades comprise the piano, they are spread out in a larger area. The arrangement of text into two blocks helps to balance the frame. The thicker, more compact lettering in the dominant top left of the screen is not too heavy for the text below it and balances with the slimmer, taller lettering at the bottom right.

The eye is drawn initially to the piano, bordered in eye-attracting red. It moves down the piano leg to "live music" where red is used again. Then the eye moves back up the piano and over to "Ziggy's" and finally down the column of text. This sequence allows the viewer to first connect with the idea of live music and then find out where it is. The specific information about place and time is available for those who wish to look further.

Unity is provided by using a border around the illustration. It is further enhanced by left-justifying the text but allowing the ends of the lines of text on the right to approach the border of the piano illustration. This pulls the illustration closer to the text.

Emphasis is created by utilizing a high-contrast illustration framed by eye-attracting color. The entire frame follows a high-contrast black and white color scheme. Too much text presented in high contrast causes the viewer to squint, but a little high-contrast text is easy to read. In this case the white text on black background advances toward the viewer, increasing readability.

A writer of electronic text does not have to be an artist to make visually interesting frames; the computer can do the drawing and apply the color. The writer must, however, provide a well conceptualized visual design to promote comfort and efficiency for the reader.

LAYOUTS

Another design strategy that translates well to computer screens is the layout. Layouts — patterns for the division of the space in a picture — give the artist a head start in applying principles of design successfully. Also, layouts help the writer break up information into chunks, which makes a frame easier to read. Nelson (1981) suggested that most layouts originate from only a few categories. Some of these layout categories adapt well to the design of computer displays. The following layouts are well suited to certain kinds of displays.

The first is the *Mondrian* layout, named after the artist Piet Mondrian. This layout consists of rectangles and/or squares of different proportions that fill a prescribed space (see Figure 6.3 upper left). The rectangles can be divided by solid lines, or their unlined edges can butt up against one another. Each rectangle contains text, pictorial information, or numbers. Some might even contain solid colors for design purposes. The Mondrian layout is useful when several interrelated tasks are to be performed at the same time.

Another format is the *picture-window* layout (Figure 6.3 upper right). In this layout the space is divided into a large box or window, and a narrow rectangle is placed above, below, or beside it. The pictorial information appears in the window, the textual information in the small rectangle. This layout is appropriate when the picture conveys the bulk of the information and the text serves as a brief clarification or anchor. The picture window works well with graphs and diagrams. (Figure 6.1 is also an example of the picture-window layout).

The next format is the *copy-heavy* layout (Figure 6.3 middle left). Only text appears in this layout, but it is used to form a pleasing and ordered design by varying the size of letters to create sequence and emphasis. This layout is good for menus or explanations of procedure.

The frame layout uses part of a pictorial design as a frame for textual information (Figure 6.3 middle right). A common variation of this layout is the "big picture." Here, the pictorial information fills the whole design space, and a small amount of text appears over a nonessential part of the picture. If the background area is too busy visually for sufficient contrast, a plain-colored box is used to hold the text. This layout is well suited for maps, diagrams, and graphs.

Figure 6.3 — Layouts

Compiled by the authors.

The last format to be discussed here is the multiple-panel or *cartoon* layout (Figure 6.3 lower right). In this layout the steps in a process are illustrated in sequence, and it is possible to display past, present, and future information all at the same time. The cartoon layout works well with flow charts, illustrated directions for the operation of equipment, and systems analyses.

An additional layout technique is the use of the shape of certain letters of the alphabet — for example, L,V,T, and Z — as patterns that help move the eye quickly through information. Placement of the objects along these patterns should not be so obvious that the letter becomes the most noticeable thing in the design; rather, the eye should speed through the information unaware of the letter.

GRIDS

Grids are another tool available to the screen designer that make the clear, concise presentation of ideas easier to achieve. Laundy and Vignelli (1980), in a publication of the American Institute of Graphic Arts, define grids as structures that provide a disciplined and consistent look while increasing production efficiency and maintaining the flexibility needed to solve a wide range of layout problems. The value of a grid is that it provides a flexible but cohesive pattern that helps the designer to establish balance, proportion, sequence, unity, and emphasis.

The computer screen is most often built with an aspect ratio of three by five, like a television screen. A grid made by dividing the screen into three columns vertically and three columns horizontally creates nine rectangles that can be used as building blocks in a variety of layouts (see Figure 6.4). Grids are particularly helpful when you need to design around system messages. After a desired layout is determined, the grid is eliminated from the screen, leaving the design behind.

Many software packages include grids as part of their graphics capability. These are easy to use because the grid can be eliminated all at once.

Grids are particularly helpful if a number of frames of information are planned on the same topic. Using the same grid as the underlying structure for each frame provides consistency and organization for the overall presentation of information.

Figure 6.4 — Layout Grids

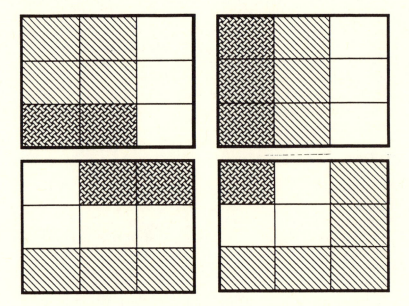

Compiled by the authors.

SPACE

A major frame-design problem is the tendency of writers to treat that screen like a manuscript page. Often, frames are packed with text and graphics. A crowded frame is difficult to read. It is hard to pinpoint information or to review significant points on a screen that is too crowded. Spacing is an important way to enhance readability. A test for good screen design in multiple page formats is suggested by Wilbert Galitz in **Handbook of Screen Format Design.** When looking at a screen all the components should be able to be identified by cues independent of textual content. If that is so, the reader's search time is significantly reduced because the reader can go right to desired information immediately (Galitz, 1985).

Colin McIntyre (1984), founding editor of the BBC's CEEFAX teletext service, states that a page of electronic text benefits most from the good use of space. He reports that the hardest thing to get new writers to recognize is that they should not jam information into a frame but should create pages with "air" in them. In a series of human factors studies, adequate spacing was found to be a more important determinant of ease of usage of information than the use of color for emphasis (Haubert and Benz, 1983).

Research done by the Electronic Text Consortium suggests two methods of providing adequate space in a frame. One is utilizing a screen-fill quotient, filling approximately 50 to 60 percent of usable space per frame. The other is developing screen-oriented messages, using one carefully edited message per frame and no more. The latter approach allows the reader to digest one thought, followed by another. Depending on the task at hand, each method works effectively to minimize clutter and maximize readability (Bamberger, 1984).

The design value of positive and negative space is a useful concept for writers of electronic text to master. Donis Dondis (1973) described positive space as those elements of a design that dominate the eye. Negative space is those design elements that are more passively displayed. It is important to pay as much attention to the negative space in a design as to the positive space. In other words, the design of the background is as significant in the overall visual effect as the arrangement of objects in the foreground. A common example of the neglect of negative space in a design is a telephone pole, unnoticed when the photograph was taken, that appears to stick out of the top of Grandma's head. Or the scalloped effect created in the right margin because the evenness of left-justified, ragged-right text was not attended to (see Figure 6.5). When a computer frame is designed, every part of the screen must be accounted for. Both positive and negative space should be treated as integral parts of the design.

Figure 6.5 — Ragged Right At Its Worst

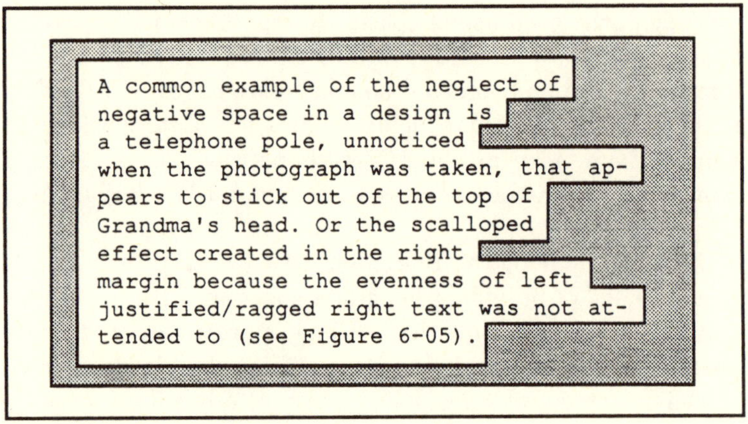

```
A common example of the neglect of
negative space in a design is
a telephone pole, unnoticed
when the photograph was taken, that ap-
pears to stick out of the top of
Grandma's head. Or the scalloped
effect created in the right
margin because the evenness of left
justified/ragged right text was not at-
tended to (see Figure 6-05).
```

Compiled by the authors.

FOCUS

There are some simple techniques to employ in order to help focus the reader on significant information on a computer display screen. Bullets and numerals set items apart. A bullet is an oversized dot placed in front of the first word in a series of related pieces of information. Bullets should be placed even with the rest of the left-justified text. A space should be left between the bullet and the word that follows (see Figure 6.6). Numerals should be placed on the line above the item to be emphasized. This makes the item clearly visible to the reader (see Figure 6.7).

Long lists create focus problems when displayed on the computer screen. In order to keep the items from appearing indistinguishable, they should be separated into groups of two (see Figure 6.8). The additional space makes all the items clearer.

Sometimes a significant fact or figure varies or changes frequently, and it is important that the viewer take note of the change. In that case utilizing a flashing text mode is useful.

Figure 6.6 — Bullet Formatting

The Hosta collection includes:
- Royal Standard Hosta
- Blue Hosta
- White Edge Hosta
- Gold Standard Hosta
- Green and White Hosta

Figure 6.7 — Numeral Formatting

1.
Rotate the drive column 38°
and align the cable pins with the
sprocket arm.
2.
Release the pressure spring
(located near the lower cover
hinge) and set meter reading.

Both figures compiled by the authors.

Flashing must be used sparingly, however, for it can be annoying and difficult to read if used too frequently in a frame.

Another technique used to create emphasis is highlighting. There are two kinds of highlighting. One is writing significant words in a color that sets them apart from the rest of the text, and the other is placing the significant words in capital letters. Sometimes both are used simultaneously. Underlining should not be used because it reduces legibility. If highlighting is used carefully, a reader can recognize the most significant information in a frame almost instantly.

Figure 6.8 — List Formatting

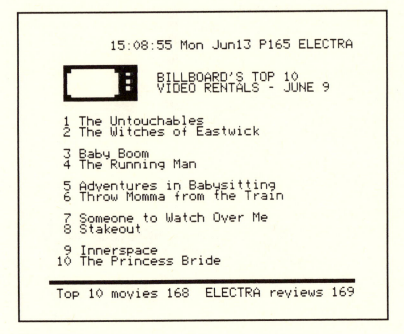

Used with permission of Great American Broadcasting.

COLOR

Color is a significant distinguishing feature of electronic text. The computer and CRT screen allow the designer great flexibility to both change and combine color — more flexibility, in fact, than practically any other medium. Color, therefore, is a basic design tool. The color in computer display is colored light. Its components are red, green, and blue — unlike the primary colors of pigment, which are red, blue, and yellow. Brightness is a major characteristic of colored light. The brightness of colors generated on the computer screen can be ranked, with white as the brightest, followed by yellow, green, blue, and red. Bright colors can be used effectively for emphasis. Less-bright colors can be used to deemphasize information. Green and yellow provide the best general visibility. Red and blue provide the lowest visibility (Galitz, 1985). Muted or subtle colors are often difficult to achieve on a CRT screen. Therefore, color has to be used judiciously in order to avoid garishness. Human factors researchers suggest that no more than two or three colors plus white be used on a screen at one time. More than that makes the frame too busy for user comfort.

Colored borders around a frame can have a unifying effect. Unity can also be achieved by using the same color in a headline and again in a trail line. Human factors research suggests that the eyes remain fixated, for brief periods, in certain positions on a screen. During these fixation pauses, information is taken in. Then rapid eye movements occur as the eye moves to another position. Little information is taken in during the rapid eye movement. It is possible that color, as well as other design strategies, could be used to create "conspicuity areas" in order to draw the eye to places for fixation pauses. This might increase the efficiency with which a reader retrieves information from a frame (Engel, 1983). There should always be some rationale for the way colors are used in a screen design. Ideally, colors should be suggested by the nature of the information being written about. When that is so, the entire message, text, and graphics work together to convey the message. Although a writer might not want to be trite, there is value in capitalizing on the viewers' culturally subjective responses to color. Writing a winter weather report in white and blue or using red and black in a graph describing profits and losses helps the viewer to reach an understanding of the material quickly because multiple mental images are brought together at once.

To convey differences, borders of contrasting colors can be used effectively — red and blue or black and white. However, complementary colors should not be used as text and background because they tend to blend together. To convey similarities, like colors can be employed — yellow and orange or black and brown. Remember, the combinations most likely to stimulate color blindness are blue and yellow and red and green.

Color contributes to a frame's readability in other ways. McIntyre (1984) suggested that the best color choices to enhance the readability of text are light blue, white, green, or yellow displayed against contrasting darker backgrounds. Screen designers usually find themselves gravitating toward favorite color combinations. Contrast is the single most important factor when making color choices. Dark colors on dark backgrounds and light colors on light backgrounds have low contrast levels and are less legible. Red and dark blue do not show up well on black, but red on yellow or white and dark blue on light blue or yellow are readable. Colors are good coding devices. If a person knows what kind of information is commonly associated with a color, then his/her search time is reduced. Headings are nicely set apart by surrounding them in a rectangle of color that contrasts with the rest of the text.

The arrangement of color for a frame of electronic text is a highly creative aspect of computer screen design; however, the writer should never lose sight of the fact that clarity and readability are the guiding design considerations.

Producing effective frames of electronic text depends a great deal on creating visual displays that clearly and simply communicate significant information to the viewer. The operational principles of visual design presented in this chapter can help create such displays because they harmonize with our subconscious channels for the internalization of visual information. Violating these principles makes it hard for people to interpret the information being presented. The computer screen is a new medium for the dissemination of information. Graphic art theory assists in making that information aesthetically pleasing, and aesthetic pleasure aides communication.

7

GRAPHICS FOR ELECTRONIC TEXT

Martin Nisenholtz, design research scientist at the Alternative Media Center, Washington, D.C., suggested four reasons to use graphics when designing frames of electronic text: first, to clarify the text; second, to enhance the text through supportive decoration; third, to represent symbolically and thereby reinforce the content of the text; fourth, to provide stylistic consistency within a single page and across content areas (Nisenholtz, 1982). Graphics can be used as a kind of shorthand to convey information that would otherwise take many lines of text to convey. But the same space constraints that make a writer turn to graphics limit the use of graphics as well. Elaborate graphics are inefficient and take up as much space as the text they are to replace. Graphics should never overpower the textual message. Text and graphics should complement each other, not fight for the reader's attention. Research done at the San Diego State University Center for Communications during the Electronic Text Consortium Project in 1984 indicated that corporate clients preferred text-only frames to frames with decorative graphics that did not contribute to the meaning of the text. Large elaborate graphics that occur repeatedly prove to be interesting at first, but subsequently annoying (Bamberger, 1984).

There are a number of types of graphics that maximize information dissemination while minimizing the use of space. For the most part these consist of simple geometric shapes that help to maintain the simplicity of a design and contribute to clean, open-looking pages that are easier to read. The graphics discussed in this chapter are signs, symbols, graphs, and diagrams.

SIGNS

Signs are a rudimentary form of graphic communication (see Figures 7.1 and 7.2). A sign stands in a one-to-one relationship to an experience (Condon, 1975). A sign has a fixed, single, concrete meaning regardless of context (Dance & Larsen, 1972).

Figure 7.1 — Sign (a)   *Figure 7.2 — Sign (b)*

Compiled by the authors.   *Compiled by the authors.*

There are three types of signs that are well suited to frame design: arbitrary, concept-related, and image-related signs (Wileman, 1980).

Signs can be represented as arbitrary graphics. These are usually abstract representations that have become so familiar that they are immediately recognized as representing the thing they describe. When using an arbitrary sign, the idea is not to create a new one but to use those that already exist and have high recognition value. Traffic signs fit into this category as do directional arrows and punctuation marks (see Figure 7.3).

Figure 7.3 — Arbitrary Signs

Compiled by the authors.

Arbitrary signs are easily reproduced because they consist of simple geometric shapes. Their value is that they call forth a clear unambiguous idea in a reader.

Concept-related signs are graphic transformations of the basic shapes found in objects. They are highly stylized representations. They can be original or familiar. All concept-related signs should be easily recognized as representations of familiar things (see Figure 7.4).

Figure 7.4 — Concept-Related Signs

Compiled by the authors.

Image-related signs are usually silhouettes or profiles of familiar objects. They are flat illustrations but are easily recognizable (see Figure 7.5). Depending on the software available and the writer's artistic ability, prepackaged images as well as original ones can be used.

Figure 7.5 — Image-Related Signs

Compiled by the authors.

SYMBOLS

A sign stands in a one-to-one relationship to an experience; a symbol suggests many possible responses (Condon, 1975). According to Suzanne Langer, signs announce and symbols remind. Symbols are simple graphic renderings that express complex ideas. A good example is the T'ai-chi tu symbolizing the yin-yang principle. One element of the design is darkness; another is lightness. The elements are not separate from one another but are parts of a whole. The T'ai-chi tu illustrates the concept that opposite balanced principles constitute duality within unity (Arnheim, 1972).

Figure 7.6 —
The T'ai-Chi Tu

Compiled by the authors.

Although creating symbols is sometimes time consuming because it requires considerable thought, symbols are a way to illustrate complex ideas with great economy.

Carl Jung felt that all cultures throughout history expressed similar motifs in their graphic illustrations. These images include visualizations of order, duality, the opposition of light and darkness, above and below surfaces, right and left, and the unification of objects in another form (Jung, 1964). It is possible that visual ideas incorporating these motifs have particular significance to human beings. People seem to be able to extrapolate from the arrangement of certain visual forms to certain life situations. Therefore, these motifs can become the building blocks for the construction of graphic symbols that powerfully and efficiently convey meaning (see Figure 7.7).

Figure 7.7 — Symbols

Compiled by the authors.

VISUAL TECHNIQUES

There are a number of visual techniques that can help a writer add meaning to the graphics in a page of electronic text. These techniques are useful for establishing tone or mood. In Figure 7.8 are some of the most useful for frame design from a larger number suggested by Donis Dondis in *A Primer of Visual Literacy* (Dondis, 1973). The application of these visual techniques can add expressiveness to the signs and symbols used to enhance textual messages written for the computer screen.

Figure 7.8a — Visual Techniques for Frame Design

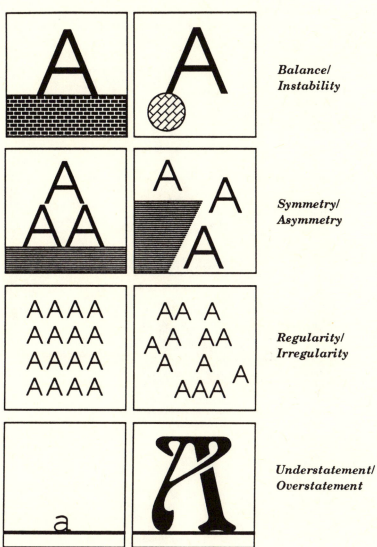

Balance/
Instability

Symmetry/
Asymmetry

Regularity/
Irregularity

Understatement/
Overstatement

Compiled by the authors.

Figure 7.8b — Visual Techniques for Frame Design

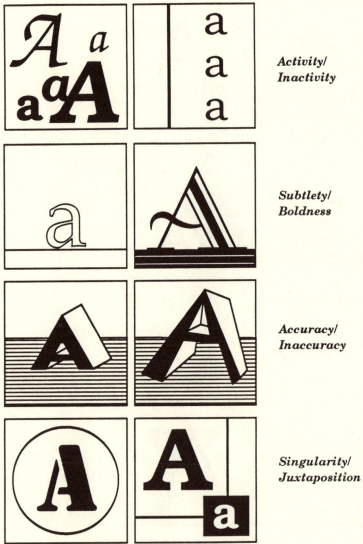

Activity/
Inactivity

Subtlety/
Boldness

Accuracy/
Inaccuracy

Singularity/
Juxtaposition

Compiled by the authors.

GRAPHS

Graphs provide a way to illustrate numerical information. Statistics are abundant in modern society. But when they are written in the text, comparisons can be obscured. Graphs make relationships between numbers visible by turning quantities into shapes. A comparison of shapes dramatizes facts by endowing them with movement or flow. Graphs can be used to make statements that can be commented about in the remaining screen space. Graphs can be divided into categories based on the kind of information they convey. Some categories well suited to electronic text application are line graphs, block graphs, and sectograms.

Line Graphs

Line graphs are used to compare how several things vary over time (see Figure 7.9). These comparisons are visualized by means of a rising and falling line that shows highs, lows, rapid

Figure 7.9 — Line Graph

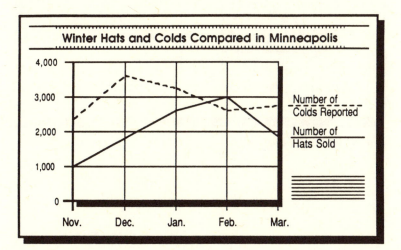

Compiled by the authors.

movement, or stability (Wileman, 1980). The statistical changes illustrated in a line graph must be substantial enough for the reader to be able to distinguish between lines. If either the points on the continuum or the lines themselves are too close together, clear differences cannot be seen and a different method of representation should be used (Holmes, 1984). Relatively thin lines are necessary so that points of reference are not obscured. Contrasting color can be used for emphasis more effectively than bold lines. Care must be taken to adjust the size of the grid in a line graph after the points of reference are plotted to ensure maximum visibility of the information. Too many grid lines obstruct a clear view. Too few grid lines don't make information easily accessible (Holmes, 1984) (see Figure 7.10).

Figure 7.10 — Too Many Grid Lines/Too Few

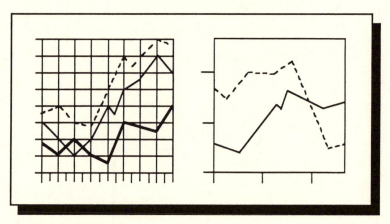

Compiled by the authors.

Block Graphs

Block graphs are used to compare quantities. There are two types of block graphs: the horizontal bar graph and the vertical bar graph. In each graph quantities are presented by bars placed on a grid. The length or height of the bars represent amounts determined by the scale of the grid (see Figure 7.11). Horizontal bar graphs compare different items during the same time frame. Vertical bar graphs measure the same item compared at different periods of time (Wileman, 1980) (see Figure 7.12). Unlike the

Figure 7.11 — Horizontal Bar Graph

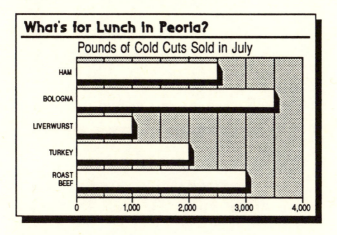

Compiled by the authors.

line graph, the block graph emphasizes totals at specific points rather than the variability of figures over time. Care should be taken to use block graphs only when the amount of numbers to be compared is relatively small. If too many comparisons are made, the bars will be too thin to have much visual impact. Bars can be overlapped in order to illustrate groupings. They can also be differentiated by filling them with contrasting textures or colors.

A unique kind of block graph is the pictogram. In a pictogram columns of little signs or symbols are used in place of bars. Each picture represents a certain quantity of the item illustrated (see Figure 7.13). Pictograms catch the eye. But they are best used to convey a general impression of quantities rather than precise

Figure 7.12 — Vertical Bar Graph

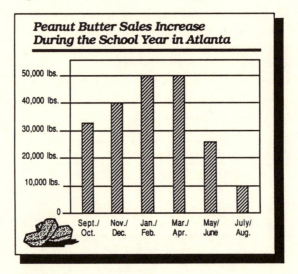

Figure 7.13 — Pictogram

Both figures compiled by the authors.

information. When constructing a pictogram, it is best to use two small items to indicate twice as many instead of one item drawn twice as big. The multiplicity of pictures conveys increased quantity much more effectively (Holmes, 1984).

Sectograms

Sectograms show how total amounts are divided up. There are three common sectograms: the pie chart, the layer chart, and the area graph. In the pie chart a circle represents the total amount. The circle is divided into triangular wedges. Each wedge represents a certain percent of the total (see Figure 7.14). A pie chart is most visually effective when fewer than ten wedges are created. Too many wedges make it hard to see comparisons clearly (Holmes, 1984). Contrasting colors or textures can be used to intensify comparisons.

Figure 7.14 — Pie Chart

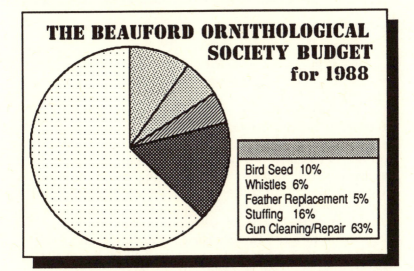

THE BEAUFORD ORNITHOLOGICAL
SOCIETY BUDGET
for 1988

Bird Seed 10%
Whistles 6%
Feather Replacement 5%
Stuffing   16%
Gun Cleaning/Repair 63%

Compiled by the authors.

A layer chart is constructed like a line graph, but areas between lines represent quantities and add up to a total amount (see Figure 7.15). The layers are differentiated by filling each with a different color or texture (Cardamone, 1981).

Figure 7.15 — Layer Chart

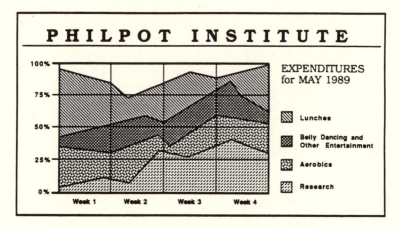

Compiled by the authors.

An area graph utilizes an outline map that orients the reader to a particular place, which is divided into sections. Each section is assigned a percentage or a total quantity (see Figure 7.16). Usually, area graphs illustrate percentages of occurrences in sections of an area (Wileman, 1980).

All graphs are constructed to a scale. A scale is a geometric projection based on the idea of a ruler. When you construct a scale, you create your own ruler consisting of equal increments. The quantity of the increments represented depends on the data you are working with. The increments of the scale are usually displayed on the left or right horizontal border of a grid. The items being measured are positioned on another border, usually the top or bottom horizontal one. The grid allows you to plot the changes in the variables (Cardamone, 1981).

Figure 7.16 — Area Graph

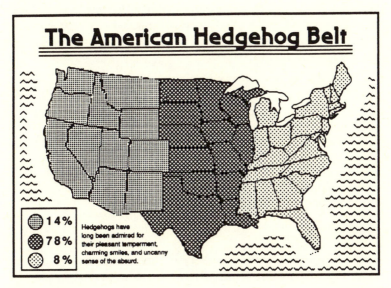

Compiled by the authors.

Most rectangular graphs can be worked out using one or ten or one hundred to one inch or one half inch. Circular graphs are handled differently. The scale for a circular graph is the increment that is used to divide the circle into wedges (Cameron, 1970).

Every graph should have an understandable title. The title can either name the subject of the graph and let readers reach their own conclusions about the data (see Figure 7.9), or it can indicate the major conclusion of the graph, pointing out the significance of the information to readers (see Figure 7.12). A compromise can be achieved by using a question as a title (see Figure 7.11). A question sets readers up but allows them to discover the answer themselves (Wileman, 1980).

All identifying information in a graph must be written briefly and consistently, and must be written within or immediately next to the grid. Letters and numbers should be written horizontally so readers don't have to bend their necks to read and should be large enough to be seen clearly. If sentences are needed to explain what a variable is, the graph should be rethought. The value of a graph lies in the speed with which the information illustrated can be understood.

TABLES

Tables are used to make numerical comparisons also. Tables are columns of numbers with subject titles arranged on a grid (see Figure 7.17). The numbers have characteristics that make them difficult to display in graphs. There are too many numbers,

Figure 7.17 — Table

INSPECTOR C51A SCHEDULE							
S	M	T	W	T	F	S	
2:30	2:30	2:30	1:00			2:30	Valve 23 check
	6:00	6:00	4:30	6:00	6:00		Flood Gate opens
7:25	7:25	7:25	7:25	7:25	7:25	7:25	Outer Switches check
8:00	8:00	8:00	8:00	8:00	8:00	8:00	Outer Switches down

Compiled by the authors.

and the differences between them are too great to chart easily. In a table the exact number is more significant than a sense of movement or flow. Time tables or tables of scheduled events are frequently used when writing electronic text.

DIAGRAMS

Diagrams are ways of visualizing physical and technical processes that are not perceptible to the eye (Herdeg, 1974). A diagram is another way of providing the maximum amount of information in the simplest and most efficient way. There are a number of kinds of diagrams that are suited to electronic presentation. They are organizational charts, flow charts, diagrams illustrating functions, and maps.

Organizational charts are visualizations of relationships between people in an organization. Most frequently organizational charts are made up of boxes and lines. The boxes represent individuals or specializations and the lines represent channels of communication (see Figure 7.18).

Figure 7.18 — Organizational Chart

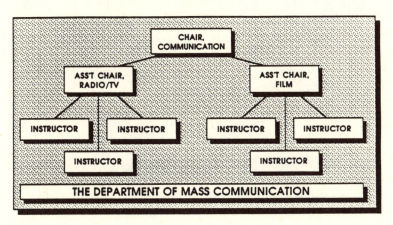

Compiled by the authors.

Flow charts illustrate the development of processes. The steps in the process are illustrated and connected in a sequence (see Figure 7.19).

Figure 7.19 — Flow Chart

Compiled by the authors.

Diagrams visualizing functions are used to illustrate, in simplified form, how a device or entity works. These diagrams provide an X-ray view or an unusual perspective that couldn't be achieved by a human in reality (see Figure 7.20).

Figure 7.20 — Diagram

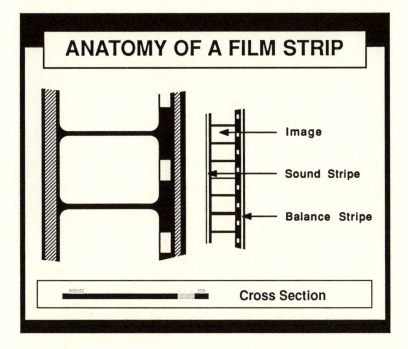

Compiled by the authors.

Maps provide a bird's eye view of how things are positioned vis-à-vis one another in a particular location (see Figure 7.21).

There are few rules that apply to creating diagrams. They are highly creative efforts reflecting the writer's understanding of the process or function described. Diagrams are called the marriage of science and art (Herdeg, 1974). In all cases the object of the creative effort is to utilize space efficiently by visualizing complex concepts instead of using strings of text to describe them. If the process can be explained visually, the text can be saved to comment on the process.

Figure 7.21 — Map

Map of the Children's Zoo

Compiled by the authors.

ERGONOMICS FOR WRITERS OF ELECTRONIC TEXT

As the number of people using computers on their jobs increased, complaints about visual and postural problems associated with using keyboard and visual display terminals began to occur. Ergonomic scientists began to study the effects of extended computer use in the workplace in order to make recommendations about how to minimize physical complaints and increase employee comfort and job satisfaction. Writers of electronic text spend a good deal of time working with computers, keyboards, and visual display terminals. So the results of ergonomic research is relevant for maximizing comfort and thereby contributing to the quality of the text.

The visual problems associated with extended use of VDT's include eye strain, blurred vision, burning or red eyes, and headaches (Grandjean, 1983). The probable reasons for these complaints are impairments in the eye's adaptation — the ability of the retina to adapt to varying illumination levels — and accommodation — the ability of the eyes to bring characters into sharp focus at various distances. Adaptation is impaired by constantly shifting back and forth from the characters on the VDT to source documents on the table next to the keyboard. Accommodation is impaired by looking at blurred characters caused by glare and flicker on the VDT (Grandjean, 1983).

There are three kinds of glare: low contrast between characters and their background on the VDT; too great contrast between the light from the VDT and the ambient light in the room; and a bright light source, like a window, next to or across from the VDT that creates reflection (Bassani, 1983). Flicker is the visible oscillation of light on the VDT. It is enhanced by high luminance of the characters and low luminance of the background and by low ambient lighting in the room and high luminance on the VDT (Grandjean, 1983).

In order to improve visual conditions so that eye strain is reduced, the following adjustments should be made: Ambient lighting in a room should be slightly lower, between 200 and 300 lux, than in the usual work setting. But the room should not be dark. Subdued ambient lighting requires additional light for source documents so that the contrast is reduced between the source documents and the VDT. The VDT should not face or be adjacent to windows or lights. If the writer wears eyeglasses, special glasses that reduce glare should be obtained (Ostberg, 1983). Finally, a writer should not work with a VDT for more than four hours a day, and no more than one hour without a break to rest the eyes (Margulies, 1983).

The postural problems that are associated with extended use of computer keyboards and VDTs are muscle fatigue in the neck, back, arms, and legs, and in some cases, injuries to the tendons in those areas. The probable reason for these problems is that people frequently work with their trunks leaning backward; necks bent forward; shoulders hunched up and held high; elbows dropped with forearms and hands held between the shoulders and elbows; and legs extended forward (Grandjean, 1983) (see Figure 7.22).

Figure 7.22 — Posture That Causes Muscle Fatigue   *Figure 7.23 — Posture That Prevents Muscle Fatigue*

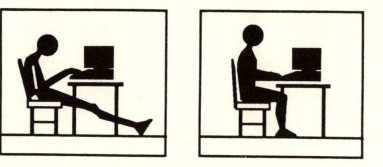

Both figures compiled by the authors.

In order to eliminate the muscle fatigue caused by this posture, the following changes in position have to occur: The neck should not be bent more than twenty degrees forward. The trunk should be kept straight. The shoulders should be relaxed and lowered. The elbows should hang down at an angle of eighty to one hundred degrees. Forearms and hands should be in a horizontal position (Grandjean, 1983) (see Figure 7.23). This position can be achieved by using a chair with adjustable height, a high back rest, and support for forearms; using a source-document support that tips the document up toward the eyes; using a table that positions the keyboard low but allows sufficient room for the knees; and using a footrest to keep the legs from sliding forward under the table (Grandjean, 1983). Creating a work environment that satisfies as many of these recommendations as possible seems to be an important prerequisite to writing electronic text.

BIBLIOGRAPHY

AP Style Book. 1980. New York: Associated Press.

Arnheim, Rudolf. 1954. *Art and Visual Perception.* Cambridge, Mass.: MIT Press.

———. 1972. *Toward a Psychology of Art.* Berkeley: University of California Press.

Aubry, Kirk. 1985. Videotex: Why should the Fortune 500 take it seriously? Proceedings of Videotex '85. New York: On-Line Publications.

Aumente, Jerome. 1983. Room at the bottom: Nobody knows the talent they'll need. *Quill 71,* 4 (April): 9-15.

Bamberger, Nancy. 1984. Videotex production: A case study. Report no. 2 of the Electronic Text Report Series. The Center for Communications, San Diego State University.

Barmack, J. E., and Sinaiko, H. W. N.d. Human factors problems in computer-generated graphic displays. Washington, D.C.: Institute for Defense Analyses, Study S-234, 166 (AD-63617C).

Barthes, R. 1972. *Image, Music, Text.* New York: Hill and Wang.

Bassani, G. 1983. NCR: From the first computer in Italy to the 1980's R&D on VDU's connected to EDP systems. In *Ergonomic Aspects of Visual Display Terminals,* eds. E. Grandjean and E. Vigliani. London: Taylor and Francis, Ltd.

Brown, C. M., Burkleo, H. V., Mangelsdorf, J. E., Olsen, R. A., and Williams, J. R. 1981. Human Factors Engineering Criteria for Information Processing Systems. Sunnyvale, Calif.: Lockheed, June.

Cameron, A. J. 1970. *A Guide to Graphs.* New York: Pergamon Press.

Cantril, Hadley, and Allport, Gordon. 1971. *Psychology of Radio.* New York: Arno Press.

Cardamone, Tom. 1981. *Chart and Graph Preparation Skills.* New York: Van Nostrand Reinhold Co.

Carey, John, and Enerson, Meryl. 1985. Staffing and training requirements for electronic text production. Report no. 7 of the Electronic Text Report Series. The Electronic Text Consortium, An Annenberg/CPB Project.

Coffey, J. L. 1961. A comparison of vertical and horizontal arrangements of alphanumeric materials. *Human Factors 3* (July): 98-98.

Condon, John. 1975. *Semantics and Communication,* 2 ed. New York: MacMillan.

Cropper, A. G., and Cropper, S. J. W. 1961. Ergonomics and Computer Display Design. *The Computer Bulletin 12*: 94-98.

Dance, Frank, and Larson, Carl. 1972. *Speech Communication: Concepts and Behavior.* New York: Holt, Rinehart and Winston.

Dondis, D. A. 1973. *A Primer of Visual Literacy.* Cambridge, Mass: MIT Press.

Engel, F. L. 1983. Information selection from visual display units. In *Ergonomic Aspects of Visual Display Terminals,* eds. E. Grandjean and E. Vigliani. London: Taylor and Francis, Ltd.

Engel, S. E., and Granda, R. E. 1975. Guidelines for Man/Display Interfaces. Poughkeepsie, N.Y.: IBM, September.

Finn, T. Andrew, and Stewart, Concetta, M. 1985. From consumer to organizational videotex applications: Will videotex find a home at the office? In ed. M. McLaughlin. *Communication Yearbook 9.* Beverly Hills, Calif.: Sage.

Foley, J. D., and Wallace, V. L. 1974. The art of natural graphic man-machine conversation. *Proceedings of the IEEE 62,* 4 (April): 462-70.

Foley, J. D., Wallace, V. L., and Chan, P. 1981. The human factors of graphic interaction: Tasks and techniques. Washington, D.C.: George Washington University, GWU-11ST-81-3, January.

Galitz, W. O. 1981, 1985. *Handbook of Screen Format Design.* Wellesley, Mass.: QED Information Sciences.

Gans, Herbert. 1980. *Deciding What's News.* New York: Random House.

Grandjean, E. 1983. Ergonomics of VDU's: A review of present knowledge. In *Ergonomic Aspects of Visual Display Terminals.* eds. E. Grandjean and E. Vigliani. London: Taylor and Francis, Ltd.

Grandjean, E., and Vigliani, E. 1983. *Ergonomic Aspects of Visual Display Terminals.* London: Taylor and Francis, Ltd.

Haber, R. N., and Wilkinson, L. 1982. Perceptual components of computer displays. *IEEE Computer Graphics and Applications 2* (3): 23-25.

Haubner, P., and Benz, C. 1983. Information display on monochrome and colour screen. Turin, Italy: Abstracts: International Scientific Conference on Ergonomic and Health Aspects in Modern Offices. November.

Herdeg, Walter. 1974. *Graphis / Diagrams.* Zurich: The Graphis Press. Distributed by Hastings House, New York.

Holmes, Nigel. 1984. *Designers' Guide to Creating Charts and Diagrams.* New York: Watson-Guptill.

International Videotex and Teletext News. 1982. Number 33, October 11.

International Videotex and Teletext News. 1984. Number 63, August.

Jonassen, David H., ed. 1985. *The Technology of Text, vol. 2,* Englewood Cliffs, N.J.: Educational Technology Publications.

Jung, Carl Gustav. 1964. *Man and His Symbols.* Garden City, N.J.: Doubleday.

Kline, David. 1983. Teletext makes viewer video pioneer. Cincinnati *Post.* 1B. Thursday, September 12.

Laundy, Peter, and Vignelli, Massimo. 1980. Graphic Design for Non-Profit Organizations. New York, NY: The American Institute of Graphic Arts.

Levine, Richard J. 1982. Broadening the business focus: Dow Jones moves into consumer data bases. *Videotex, Key to the Information Revolution.* New York: On-Line Publications.

Marcus, A. 1982. Managing facts and concepts. Washington, D.C.: National Endowment for the Arts, Design Arts Program.

Margulies, F. 1983. Trade union aspects and experiences with work on VDU's. In *Ergonomic Aspects of Visual Display Terminals.* E. Grandjean and E. Vigliani. London: Taylor and Francis, Ltd.

Markower, J. 1981. *Office Hazards.* Washington, D.C.: Tilden Press.

McIntyre, Colin. 1984. *The Practical Guide to Teletext and Videotex.* London: Strauss-Hill Communications. Miller, I. M. 1979. A Tutorial in Computer Graphics. Paper presented at the annual meeting of the Human Factors Society, Boston, October.

Miller, L. A., and Thomas, Jr., J. C. 1976. Behavioral issues in the use of interactive systems. Yorktown, N.Y.: IBM, Research Report RC 6326, December.

Mitchell, C., and Miller, R. A. 1983. Design Strategies for Computer-Based Information Displays in Real-Time Control Systems. *Human Factors 25* (4): 1-17.

Nelson, R. H. 1981. *The Design of Advertising.* Dubuque, Iowa: William Brown Co.

Newman, W. M., and Sproull, R. F. 1979. *Principles of Interactive Computer Graphics.* New York: McGraw-Hill.

Nisenholtz, Martin. 1982. Designing for teletext and videotex: Two case studies. *Electronic Publishing Review 2* (3): 199-209.

Ostberg, O. 1983. Accommodation and visual fatigue in display work. In *Ergonomic Aspects of Visual Display Terminals,* eds. E. Grandjean and E. Vigliani. London: Taylor and Francis. Ltd.

Parrish, R. N., Gates, J. L., Munger, S. J., and Sidorsky, R. C. 1981. Development of design guidelines and criteria for user/operator transactions with battlefield automated systems, volume IV: Provisional guidelines and criteria for the design of user/operator transactions (draft final report, phase I). Alexandria, Va.: U.S. Army Research Institute.

Plotnik, Arthur. 1982. *The Elements of Editing.* New York: MacMillian.

Poulton, E. C., and Brown, C. H. 1968. Rate of comprehension of an existing teleprinter output and of possible alternatives. *Journal of Applied Psychology 52* (1): 16-21.

Ramsey, H. R., and Atwood, M. E. 1979. Human factors in computer systems: A review of the literature. Englewood, Colo.: Science Applications, September.

Reilly, S., and Roach, J. 1984. Improved visual design for graphics display. *IEEE Computer Graphics and Applications 4* (2): 42-51.

———. 1986. Designing human/computer interfaces: A comparison of human factors and graphic arts principles. *Educational Technology 26* (1): 36-40.

Roach, J., Hartson, H. R., Ehrich, R. W., Yunten, T., and Johnson, H. 1982. DMS — A comprehensive system for managing human-computer dialogues. Proceeding of Human Factors in Computing Systems, ACM, Gaithersberg, Md., March.

Roach, J., Pittman, J. A., Reilly, S. S., and Savarse, J. 1982. Visual design consultant. Paper presented at the International Conference on Cybernetics and Society, Seattle, Washington, October.

Sackman, H. 1970. *Man-Computer Problem Solving.* Princeton, N.J.: Averback Publishers.

Schneiderman, B. 1979. Human factors in designing interactive systems. *Computer 12* (12): 9-19.

Schutz, H. G. 1961. An evaluation of methods for presentation of graphic multiple trends: Experiment III. *Human Factors 3* (July): 108-119.

Shields, N. 1980. Spacelab display design and command usage Guidelines. Moffet Field, Calif.: NASA AMES, Technical Report MFSC-PROC-711A, April.

Smith, S. L. 1981. Man-machine interface (MMI) requirements definition and design guidelines: A progress report. Bedford, Mass: MITRE, February.

Strunk, Williams, and White, E. B. 1979. *The Elements of Style.* New York: MacMillan.

Taylor, I. A. 1960. Perception and visual communication, perception and design. In *Research Principles and Practices in Visual Communication,* eds. J. Ball and F. Pyres. Washington, D.C.: Association for Educational Communication and Technology.

Tedford, W. H. S., Berquist, S. L., and Flynn, W. E. 1979. The size-color illusion. *Journal of General Psychology 97:* 145-149.

Thomas, John L., and Schneider, Michael L. 1986. *Human Factors in Computer Systems.* Norwood, N.J.: Ablex Publishing Corp.

Truckenbrod, Joan. 1988. *Creative Computer Imaging.* Englewood Cliffs, N.J.: Prentice Hall.

Tullis, T. S. 1981. An evaluation of alphanumeric, graphic, and color information displays. *Human Factors 23* (5): 541-550.

UPI Broadcast Style Book. 1979. New York: United Press International.

UPI Reporter. 1983. April 15.

Vignelli, Massimo. 1978. Grids: Their meaning and use for federal designers. Washington, D.C.: Federal Design Library. December.

Walker, David. 1985. *Financial Times.* August 16.

Wileman, Ralph E. 1980. *Exercises in Visual Thinking.* New York: Hastings House.

Williges, B., and Williges, R. 1981. Technical report prepared for engineering psychology programs, Office of Naval Research, ONR Contract Number N00014-810-k-0143, September.

Williges, R. C., and Williges, B. H. 1982. Human-computer dialogue design considerations. Proceeding of the IFAC/IFIP/IFOPS/IEA Conference. Analysis, Design, and Evaluation of Man-Machine Systems, Baden-Baden, FRG International Federation of Automatic Controls, September.

Winter, Peter. 1985. *Common Sense Videotex and Teletext: The North American Market.* New York: Strauss Hill Communications.

INDEX

ABOUT THE AUTHORS

HILARY GOODALL is a teletext veteran. Some ten years involvement in the operational side of electronic publishing make her one of the leading experts in teletext production and design in the United States.

Ms. Goodall is director of teletext development for Great American Broadcasting in Cincinnati. She was responsible for starting the ELECTRA service, the nation's first and longest-running commercial teletext venture. Previously, she was chief subeditor with the BBC's CEEFAX service in London.

Her background is in print journalism. Before joining the BBC, Ms. Goodall was a desk editor for various British newspapers and magazines. She has a degree in history from the University of Kent.

SUSAN SMITH REILLY is associate professor and director of the mass communication program in the Department of Communication at Miami University, Oxford, Ohio. Dr. Reilly received her Ph.D. in communication from the Pennsylvania State University in 1978. Her research interests include visual information, new information technologies, and broadcast writing.